PRAISE FOR BRETT DUFUR'S GUIDEBOOKS

"Whether a first-time mountain biker or a seasoned veteran, the new Show Me Mountain Biking guidebook will first and foremost impress you with its detail. The author has included everything from where to park, to which flowers are likely to bloom during your ride. It also prepares you for extended adventures with important information on lodging, camping and dining.

Congratulations to Brett Dufur on a job well done. Show Me Mountain Biking is a valuable resource that every Missouri cyclist should own."

— *Steve Pittman, Editor*
Cycle St. Louis

"Where most guidebook authors finish, Dufur is just getting warmed up. . . . This book contains fun facts not even a history teacher would know."

— *Chuck MacDonald*
St. Louis Times

"The gorgeous photography is the best by far I've seen in any mountain bike guidebook — ever. I especially enjoy the extensive sections covering history, flora and fauna. This book is as visually pleasing as it is informative."

— *Jennifer Kulier, Associate Editor*
Cycle St. Louis

"Dufur, a reporter by schooling, has an eye for stories. . . . And after a long jaunt through Latin America, he knows the value of a good guidebook. "

— *Lisa Groshong*
Columbia Daily Tribune

D0907354

OTHER BOOKS IN THE SHOW ME MISSOURI SERIES

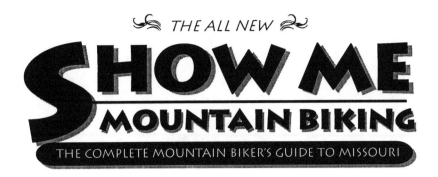

THE ALL NEW
SHOW ME
MOUNTAIN BIKING
THE COMPLETE MOUNTAIN BIKER'S GUIDE TO MISSOURI

By Brett Dufur

One and all are possessed with the spirit of motion.

— Mary Dodge
From her classic tale Hans Brinker

Illustrations by Bob Bliss

Photographs by Margo "Dirt Gypsy" Carroll

Maps by Cartographic Works

Project support by Pebble Publishing staff: Addie & R.C. Adams, Brian Beatte, Tawnee Brown, Brett Dufur, Daisy Dufur, Pippa Letsky and Hope Wagner.

Maps by Cartographic Works: Lawrence "Ted" Twenter, Robert Cline and Elizabeth Touchette.

Photographs by Margo Carroll/M2 Images

ISBN 1-891708-02-3 16.95

Pebble Publishing, P.O. Box 2, Rocheport, MO 65279
Phone: (573) 698-3903 Fax: (573) 698-3108
Email: pebble@showmestate.com

Printed by Walsworth Publishing, Marceline, Missouri, USA

DEDICATION

I would like to dedicate my work in this book to my mom, Shirley Carroll, who's overwhelming generosity and kindness in life continue to move and inspire me.

— Margo Carroll

ACKNOWLEDGMENTS

This book is the culmination of countless hours of pedal time and research. The following people certainly deserve the credit for making it the complete guide that it is. I'm indebted to the following people for sharing years of pedaling experience: Amber and Bart Bachura, Cathy Byland, Bart Childers, Rob Cline, Raymond Cox, Tim Fox, Brian Hossfeld, Sheila Huddleston, Ron Jacobs, Teresa Kight, Jenny Landseerd, Randy Long, Dan Maijala, Joe Martin, Brad Mitchell, Fred Pearson, Ron, Mike Rago, Jeff Scheble, Deb Schnack, Damon Sprague, Andrew Stokes, Damien Wardien and Brian Weed.

Many reviewers also contributed valuable comments. They include: Heather Atkinson, Bert Asher, Margo Carroll, Nancy Feakes, Teresa Kight, Jenny Kulier, Bruce Linders, Deb Schnack, Andrew Stokes and Terry Whaley and many others. Also, a special thanks goes to Steve Pittman, the editor of *Cycle St. Louis*, who is a long time friend and fellow pen and pedal pusher.

To photographer and "dirt gypsy" Margo Carroll, I am extremely thankful. Her photographs bring the pages of this book alive. Thanks for your ideas and for sharing your "eye." Thanks also go out to Terry Barner and Peggy Welch for their splendid photographs.

A special thanks also goes out to Michelle, Brian and the rest of the staff at Pebble who so naturally said "He's not in" so I could spend one more day out of the office riding single track or crunching out yet another day's worth of work on this book. Thanks. To Tawnee and the critters, I'm back. Thanks for helping me throughout this project.

The greatest thanks of all goes to the Missouri Department of Conservation, Forest Service and Department of Natural Resources personnel and countless volunteers who make these trails happen.

TABLE OF CONTENTS

Rides:

ST. LOUIS & EASTERN REGION . . . 37

COLUMBIA & CENTRAL REGION . . . 71

KANSAS CITY & WESTERN REGION . . . 109

SPRINGFIELD & OZARK MOUNTAINS REGION ... 137

ROLLA & OZARK HIGHLANDS REGION ... 163

OZARK TRAIL ... 185

SOUTHEAST REGION ... 213

Katrina Miller kisses the sky at Castlewood State Park.

FOREWORD BY THE AUTHOR

Missouri is blessed with some amazingly diverse geography, which leads to several lifetimes' worth of single-track adventure. Within Missouri, we have more than 80 trails to choose, from Ozark highland trails to technically challenging steep creek drainages and even the longest rails-to-trails project in the United States.

So gearheads and outdoor-types rejoice. Forget those midnight drives across Kansas to get to Colorado's Rockies. Forget about the Appalachian Trail and the Smokies. Flip some pages and find your adventures close to home, without losing valuable playtime or tankloads of gas. Missouri is blessed with some incredible single track and this book will show you where to find it.

In this book, Missouri mountain biking is divided into different regions, based upon geography and the population centers around the state: St. Louis, Columbia, Kansas City, Springfield, Rolla and the southeast region, which encompasses most of the Ozark Trail.

Quite simply, most of the good stuff is close to or south of the Missouri River. That's because when the glaciers retreated 10,000 to 2 million years ago, they flattened northern Missouri, and began to recede near where the Missouri River now flows. That left our central and southern hills and Ozarks full of all of those bumps, drops, zigs and zags we love to call home. No matter where you are, there is surely a gorgeous setting and a great workout nearby.

Countless smiles and spills culminated into this book, where I have highlighted what feels like a record of 80 mountain bike rides. This surpasses the scope of trails outlined in Steve Henry's 1993 edition of *The Mountain Biker's Guide to the Ozarks*, which offers 36 Missouri trails, and Brian Mais and Gary Barnett's 1995 guidebook entitled *The Fatheads Guide to Mountain Biking Missouri*, which highlights 35 trails.

This book has taken me to the best natural areas Missouri offers—and, oh my, there are quite a few. Basically, there is some prime off-road biking within easy reach of every metropolitan area in the state, as well as many choice daytrip and weekend getaways hidden deep within the Ozarks. In addition to up-to-date information, great maps and reliable directions, there are a couple of articles included in this book for those rainy day armchair odysseys. If you only have time to read one, I recommend the article on page 20 about what to do when you meet up with a rider on horseback.

I have exhaustively researched trails, interviewed trail gypsies, scrounged for maps and old documents and hounded Conservation and Department of Natural Resources officials hoping to get the definitive word on trails open to mountain bikers. It has been a true education. In my quest, I worked with many administrative-types who thought mountain biking had something to do with motocross. Oftentimes, I would have to request information on equestrian trails instead of mountain biking trails, since an alarming number of people at area visitors centers and such don't understand exactly what mountain biking is.

We are on the mere cusp of being understood by civilization at large. Because of the infancy of our sport, remember that your positive actions today may very well help set a positive stage for tomorrow's policies regarding us dirt-chewing bikers. Remember too, that we must continue to educate the general public and policy makers about this fun, low-impact and healthy sport. We have a long way to go.

Take care out there and don't forget—always invite a friend— it's the best way to increase stewardship of our beautiful outdoors and besides, they'll probably buy you lunch!

See you out there!

Brett Dufur
The Author

INTRODUCTION

Whether a first-time mountain biker or a seasoned veteran, the new Show Me Mountain Biking guidebook will first and foremost impress you with its detail. In the pages that follow, you will find an outstanding body of information on the mountain bike trails and off-road paths of Missouri.

The author has included everything from where to park, to which flowers are likely to bloom during your ride. Show Me Mountain Biking can also help you prepare for an extended adventure with important information on lodging, camping and dining.

What this book (or any book) cannot provide, however, is the common horse sense required for cycling in remote wilderness areas. Indeed, the solitude and rugged beauty that draws thousands each year to Missouri's trails can also lull the unprepared into dangerous situations.

In addition to reading this guidebook, users should prepare themselves for each ride by considering their physical limitations, the weather, and the condition of their equipment. In very remote areas, carry plenty of water, a compass, a map and the tools needed to accomplish minor repairs and to fix multiple flat tires. Lastly, I recommend always riding with a buddy. This will add to your safety on the trail, and it's a lot more fun.

Congratulations to Brett Dufur on a job well done. Show Me Mountain Biking is a valuable resource that every Missouri cyclist should own.

Steve Pittman
Editor, *Cycle St. Louis*

ABBREVIATIONS:

To save space throughout the book, I've used several abbreviations—some more traditional than others.

B&B for Bed and Breakfast.
FR for Forest Road.
MTB for mountain bike or mountain biking.
DNR for Department of Natural Resources.
Hwy for highway.
MDOC for the Missouri Department of Conservation.
MTNF for Mark Twain National Forest.
GPS for global positioning system.
CCC for Civilian Conservation Corps.

PREPARING TO RIDE IN BACKCOUNTRY MISSOURI:

By Jennifer Kulier
Associate Editor, *Cycle St. Louis*

When riding trails in central Missouri, some self-sufficiency is necessary. Familiarity with a trail map is essential. Trails are usually well marked, but keep your eye out for trail markers, especially when riding fast. Carry a few tools, extra water and a snack. This isn't Castlewood, and you won't find a fellow mountain biker around every bend if you break your rear derailleur. You may not see another mountain biker at all. Expect to see families out for day hikes and maybe a hunter on an ATV. You'll have the trail to yourself, especially in winter.

It's also a good idea to bring a pair of jeans and a jacket to wear over your bike clothes for the car ride. A run into John's Bait and Tackle in your Lycra and Brikos can get you some funny "You ain't from around here" looks from the denim and camo crowd.

RULES OF THE TRAIL:

The following list is a compilation of rules common to most state and federal lands. Please respect them and be aware of any additional rules that might pertain to a given area.

- ✓ Always wear a helmet.
- ✓ Please keep pets on leashes at all times.
- ✓ Only ride on trails marked open for mountain bikes.
- ✓ Yield to all hikers and equestrians.
- ✓ When permitted, camp at least 100 feet from the trail. Leave it in better shape than you found it.
- ✓ Treat all water before drinking.
- ✓ Always notify someone of your trip itinerary.
- ✓ Always read the bulletin board at the trailhead.
- ✓ Call ahead for the latest trail conditions.
- ✓ Use caution when crossing streams.
- ✓ Do not build fires on the edges of bluffs, on glades or in caves. Never leave a fire unsupervised.
- ✓ Completely bury all human waste at least 100 feet from the trail.
- ✓ Some parks prohibit riding in wet conditions.
- ✓ Enjoy plants in their natural settings. Do not collect plants.
- ✓ Be considerate of others, respect the rights of private landowners and remember that solitude is also a resource to be protected.

IF YOU PLAN to TAKE YOUR
MOUNTAIN BiKe
iNto the GReAt OutDOORS
DON't BEHAVE LiKe...
Wild WiLLy!™
LeARN AND PRActice the
i.M.B.A.
iNterNAtioNAL MOUNtAiN BicYCLiNG ASSOC.
RuLeS of the TRAIL!

(IMBA RULES OF TRAIL CARTOONS) ©1992 Curt Evans & IMBA

BEFORE YOU HIT THE TRAIL

Before you start exploring, please take a moment to review the International Mountain Bicycling Association (IMBA) rules of the trail. Do your part to maintain trail access by observing the following rules. IMBA's mission is to promote environmentally sound and socially responsible mountain bicycling.

1. RIDE ON OPEN TRAILS ONLY. Respect trail and road closures (ask if not sure), avoid possible trespass on private land, obtain permits or other authorization as may be required. Federal and state Wilderness areas are closed to cycling. The way you ride will influence trail management decisions and policies.

LeAVe No tRACe!

RiDe ON OPeN tRAiLS ONLY!

CoNtRoL YouR BiCYCLe!

2. LEAVE NO TRACE. Even on open (legal) trails, you should not ride under conditions where you will leave evidence of your passing, such as after a rain. Practice low-impact cycling. This also means staying on existing trails and not creating new ones. Don't cut switchbacks. Pack out as much as you pack in.

3. CONTROL YOUR BICYCLE! Inattention for even a second can be dangerous. Obey bicycle speed limits and other rules.

4. ALWAYS YIELD TRAIL. Make known your approach well in advance. A friendly greeting or bell is considerate and works well; don't startle others. Show your respect when passing by slowing to a walking pace or even stopping. Anticipate other trail users around corners or in blind spots.

5. NEVER SPOOK ANIMALS. All animals are startled by an unannounced approach, a sudden movement or a loud noise. This can be dangerous for you, others and the animals. Give animals extra room and time to adjust to you. When passing horses use special care and follow directions from the horseback riders (ask if uncertain). Running cattle and disturbing wildlife is a serious offense. Leave gates as you found them, or as marked.

6. PLAN AHEAD. Know your equipment, your ability and the area in which you are riding—and prepare accordingly. Be self-sufficient at all times, keep your equipment in good repair, and carry necessary supplies for changes in weather or other conditions. Always wear a helmet and appropriate safety gear.

KEEP TRAILS OPEN BY SETTING A GOOD EXAMPLE OF ENVIRONMENTALLY SOUND AND SOCIALLY RESPONSIBLE OFF-ROAD CYCLING.

ALWAYS YieLD tRAiL!

PLAN AHeAD!

NeveR SPook ANiMALS!

COMMONLY ASKED MTB QUESTIONS:

1. I'M JUST GETTING INTO THIS. WHAT KIND OF BIKE SHOULD I GET? Forget the character on Saturday Night Live who said "Darling, it's better to look good than feel good." Make sure you get the bike you *need*, which is usually less expensive than the bike you *want*. Be serious about how you are going to use it. If you are going hard-core off-roading definitely go full suspension. Going with just a front shock for occasional forays off-road will save you hundreds of dollars over full suspension. And if you're budget conscious, there's nothing that says you *must have* suspension. Heck, if you'll probably spend most of your time on bike paths, even consider a hybrid, which gives you upright comfort to hit the longer bike paths around the state.

2. WHAT IS YOUR FAVORITE TRAIL? Trails are like fishing holes—you have different favorites for different reasons. Proximity and work-out level both play a part in selecting a trail to fit your mood. I certainly prefer "anything south." I love the Ozarks whether it's 5 below or a sparkling 80 degrees. I recommend doing as many daytrip and weekend getaways as you can to really appreciate the abundance of trails Missouri has to offer. Variety is the spice of life.

3. HOW SHOULD I TRAIN? Certainly nothing can replace pedal time. But you can certainly get on the right track by eating right, focusing on cardiovascular work-outs and making sure your bike is in tip-top shape.

4. HOW WILL I KNOW IF A TRAIL IS OPEN TO MOUNTAIN BIKES? This is certainly the touchy subject of the '90s, as areas set aside for hiking and conservation are finding an increasing number of mountain bikers showing up at their trailheads. All of the trails in this book are 100 percent MTB legal. I've included notes for areas where both trails for MTBs and trails prohibiting MTBs are present. Things do change, however. Just ask, and you'll get the whole scoop.

5. ANY OTHER SUGGESTIONS? Don't forget to check with local bike clubs (which are listed in the back) and join them for some unforgettable outdoor experiences. Learn from the old sages and know your own abilities and limitations!

18 — SHOW ME MOUNTAIN BIKING

GEAR LIST:

YOU:
Good attitude • Open mind
2 one-quart water bottles
    or similar water carrier
Powerbars or candy bars
Biking shorts • Loose-fitting shirt
Rain jacket • Emergency smile
Sun protection
Bandanas (work for towels, sun protec-
tion, coffee filters, bad hair days, etc.)
Camera & extra film
Small personal first aid kit
Sunglasses/Eye protection

YOUR BIKE:
Tuned-up bike • Helmet
2 extra tubes
Pump/Slime patch goop
Small tool kit
Multi-tool or Leatherman
Small seat pouch
Spare master chain link
    or extra chain

IN YOUR CAR:
Emergency cash or credit card
Towel & biodegradable soap
Toilet paper • Duct tape
Small flashlight • Pocket knife
Hacky sack • Favorite snacks
Good road-trip tapes

FOR OVERNIGHT TRIPS:
Lightweight sleeping bag
Foam sleeping pad & tent

FOR WINTER TRIPS ADD:
Wool sweater or pile jacket
Warm gloves & wind breaker
Polypropylene socks

NOTES:
All Missouri bike shops are listed in the
back of this book. • Bring asthma in-
halers and other medications in clearly
marked containers. • Keep extra cloth-
ing, food, water and tools in your car.

REMEMBER:
Nothing weighs nothing. The less you
bring on your ride, the bigger your
smile. • This isn't an expensive sport
unless you want it to be. Before you
lighten your Visa, ask. Most items can
be borrowed from fellow gearheads. •
Thoreau was really talking about outdoor recreation when he said,
"Simplify, simplify."

EQUESTRIANS AND CYCLISTS:

CAN WE GET ALONG?

By Theo Stein

Perhaps no animal has meant as much to the advance of human culture as the horse. Once the horse was domesticated, its trainability, strength and speed afforded human cultures a quantum leap forward. The horse became beast of burden, transportation and a devastating weapon of war. On the broad back of this noble beast, kingdoms were gained and lost. Today, because of the relative fortune required to purchase and maintain a horse, equestrians are often landed citizens: people with clout.

Therein lies the rub: mountain biking is a new sport whose devotees are relatively young and not rich. We all wish it were otherwise, but money talks. It may be the horse owners who will be able to pull the right strings when conflicts arise. Therefore, it behooves (sorry) us to make friends of equestrians.

But this issue is more than just a turf battle over trails between us young turks and them establishment-types. It also has to do with safety. On the back of a startled horse, attached only by gripping thighs, a rider is in an extremely precarious position. And to a horse, a mountain biker screaming around a blind corner at Warp Nine looks like a nightmare from hell: alien, silent and horrifyingly fast.

While hiker-cyclist conflicts provoke most land access battles, chance encounters between horses and bicycles pose a far greater threat of injury and death. A horse, by design, is a nervous, cautious beast. Mountain bikers are, more or less, risk-takers. When these two very different users meet unexpectedly on the trail, the results are sometimes disastrous.

Deb Carano, a rider for 26 years and world-class equestrienne racer from New England, believes that the majority of unpleasant horse-bicycle incidents arise from our own ignorance about how this herbivore perceives its world. When faced with potential danger, humans may choose to fight or flee. Horses have one response, and that's flight — right now.

One of Deb's housemates, Tunde Ludanye, has studied equine behavior and sensory perception. She says that if self-preservation is the first law of nature, it's also the last word in horse sense. The horse has an inbred fear of being eaten. It is known to be the fastest animal in the world at distances over 50 yards, but within that distance, it is vulnerable to ambush artists like lions and wolves. That first 50 yards is crucial. To gain this ever-important head start, a horse depends on an amazing sensory system—a 360-degree field of vision and ears that swivel a full 180 degrees.

Tucci says it's possible to understand a horse's seemingly irrational reactions as natural wariness. Remember, it's an animal of wide open spaces, not twisty single track. Tucci notes that a horse instinctively fears small, tight, dark places, like trailers, as places where a horse-eater may be lurking. A tight trail in deep woods may also make a horse nervous.

The only way to calm a spooked horse is to convince it that there is nothing to fear. A trained animal takes its cues from its rider. A startled horse under a startled rider is a dangerous combination. A startled horse under a calm rider is less so.

One of the most volatile elements in the mix is that every animal is different. "My horse Hardin is bomb-proof," she said. "The previous owner used to take him hunting and shoot a gun off his back." Deb and Hardin also used to tag along behind a racer-friend when he trained in the woods. "Hardin loved it. He would just fall in behind the bike and away we'd go. But even with a bomb-proof horse, if you startle it, it's going to shy."

While a horse is a large animal, it is also quite fragile. "There are a number of things that can happen to a horse, just like with any human athlete." A spooked horse, madly dashing over hill and dale, can easily pop a tendon, tear a ligament, break a cannon bone, or twist a fetlock, which is the equine equivalent of spraining our wrist. Any of these injuries entail a long-term recovery and big-time veterinarian costs. A severe injury may oblige the owner to euthanize the animal, which is part cherished friend and part investment. Any rider who has had a horse injured or put down after being spooked by cyclists is sure to hit the warpath against mountain bike access.

But the party most in danger during unexpected confrontations is the person riding a spooked horse.

"Typically horses weigh 1,000 pounds and up," she said. "When you startle a horse, its instinctive reaction is flight, and that's when people get hurt." The most common injuries, Deb says, are broken shoulders and wrists and lungs punctured by broken ribs. But more serious injuries do happen. Deb has seen one rider break his back after getting thrown. She also knows of riders who were killed after they were thrown into a tree or a stone wall. Even a sudden sideways movement in the woods may result in the rider being crushed against a tree or clotheslined by a low-hanging limb.

HOW TO AVOID CONFLICT

Approaching a horse and rider suddenly from the rear is the most perilous type of meeting. Popping up in a horse's face will certainly scare the bejeesus out of the animal, but at least the rider can quickly identify you and act accordingly.

A horse is likely to sense a cyclist approaching from the rear before its rider, and will instinctively perceive that cyclist as a threat to its safety. This is why it is vital that you make your presence known to the rider.

"No matter which way you approach, it's critical you alert the rider as soon as possible," Deb said. The best thing to do, she said, is to slow to a crawl or stop and ask the rider for instructions. Don't be bashful and don't wait until you get close. Just sing out, "Rider back. May we pass?"

The rider may tell you to pass, or to wait while she moves the horse off the trail. The rider may just need to turn the animal around so it can look you over. With a skittish animal or inexperienced rider, you may have to dismount and move off the trail yourself.

Deb also recommends you outfit your bike with a bell, even a tiny, tin kitty bell under your seat. "That may give the horse and rider the split-second warning they need to buy time for everybody involved."

But the most important thing is to let the equestrian control the flow of events. The horse needs to know the rider is in charge. "Ask the rider for instructions no matter what," she said. "They will appreciate it."

Anticipating incidents is the best way to avoid nasty accidents. Keep your eyes open for horse sign on the trail. A 1,200 pound animal shod with steel shoes leaves tracks on everything short of asphalt. Even then, manure piles should alert you that you're sharing the trail with an animal.

If you suspect there's a horse somewhere ahead, consider riding elsewhere. If it's your training day, do ride elsewhere. Otherwise, proceed with caution and make noise as you go.

Despite having a bomb-proof horse familiar with bicyclists, Deb said that she tries to keep Hardin away from mountain bikes whenever possible, more so because she's afraid of how bikers will act than how Hardin will.

"I like trail riding, but it's not relaxing," she said. Given that a horse may spook at the sight of a deer, a few anxious moments per ride in the woods is the norm. Knowing that mountain bikes may be in the area ratchets up the tension level dramatically.

"To be honest, I don't go to areas where I can expect to run into them [mountain bikers]," she said. "The potential for disaster is just too great where the horse and rider are concerned. I've been there and it's not fun."

SHOW RESPECT AND UNDERSTANDING

That admission begs the question: "Can we get along?" Yes, if we show respect and know what horses do and what they need. If we don't do that, then I think we're going to be denied access to a lot of great mountain biking. And who wants that?

Reprinted from IMBA Trail News

MORE HORSE TIPS:

1. If a horse is crossing a bridge, cyclists should always wait for the horse to finish.
2. Cyclists should never approach a horse while it is crossing creeks or other water.
3. When calling to the horserider to alert them of your presence, remember it is best not to holler or yell excitedly, but to speak calmly. If the cyclist is some distance from the horse, a loud but calm voice should be used. There is nothing wrong with a "Hello, it's really a nice day for riding, isn't it?" The more an approaching cyclist talks when passing, the more the horse will realize it is just a human being on a strange-looking contraption.

By Margo Ems, Lincoln, NE
Copyright International Mountain Bicycling Association

U.S. FOREST SERVICE
MARK TWAIN NATIONAL FOREST
RANGER DISTRICTS

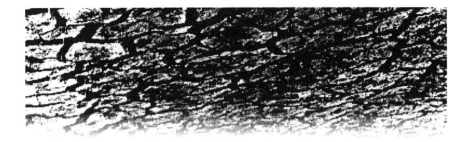

INTRODUCTION TO THE MARK TWAIN NATIONAL FOREST

The next few pages serve as an introduction to the Mark Twain National Forest. Many of the best MTB trails in Missouri are located on the U.S. Forest Service's land. You will hear these areas referred to in many ways. If you understand the chain of command, it will help you to avoid confusion.

The U.S. Department of Agriculture oversees the U.S. Forest Service, which oversees the Mark Twain National Forest, which is managed by the ranger districts shown on the left.

The name Mark Twain National Forest is a little misleading because, although there is a "national forest," there are actually nine separate parcels of land that make up the Mark Twain Forest. Since these Mark Twain National Forest Areas are peppered throughout several MTB regions, a brief overview of what the forest is will make the rest of the book make a whole lot more sense.

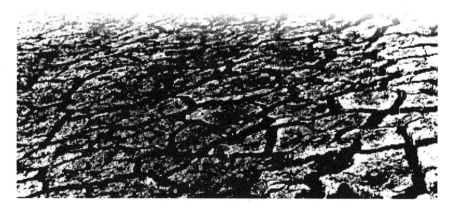

INTRODUCTION TO MARK TWAIN NATIONAL FOREST

The Mark Twain National Forest is located in southern Missouri. The forest lies mostly within the Ozark Plateau dotted with remnant hills from this country's oldest mountains, the Ozarks. It encompasses 1,493,198 acres, with many streams fed by some of the largest springs in the country. Within the MTNF, seven congressionally designated wilderness areas cover 63,000 acres and there are 28 developed campgrounds.

. . . mountain biking is permitted on MTNF roads and trails unless specifically posted as closed to such use . . . the exception being that all wilderness areas are closed to mountain bikers . . .

The Mark Twain National Forest is a forest of surprises. There are glimpses of West Virginia, Pennsylvania, Virginia and even a little Arizona and California. The Mark Twain is composed of 12 ranger districts and separated by privately owned land.

Driving past fields of freshly harvested crops and sun-browned grass, one may wonder where is the green of the forest? A forest signpost says "turn here" and within a very short distance, there will be a towering oak and hickory sheltering petite dogwood and sassafras.

Created in the 1930s by legislation and with the reintroduction of deer and turkey in 1945, today it is hard to see the destruction caused by post–Civil War over-logging and frequent wildfires. Stretching from the St. Francis mountains in the southeast to the Ozarks in the southwest, the Mark Twain contains a variety of topography and wildlife.

Aside from offering some of the best MTB trails and hiking trails in the state, floating is also a popular activity here, with 350 miles of floatable streams.

The MTNF is a maze of hiking trails from the easiest and most leisurely to the more strenuous, hard-core hiker's trails, such as the

500-mile Ozark Trail, with completed sections and some still in the planning phase. This trail will eventually stretch from St. Louis through the Mark Twain National Forest into Arkansas.

The Mark Twain National Forest offers sights, sounds and experiences to be remembered for a lifetime. Canoeing down the fast-flowing Current River, kayaking the white water on the St. Francis River, looking into a valley atop a "tough" climb or any number of other outdoor experiences, the Mark Twain is ready for you.

QUICK MOUNTAIN BIKING OVERVIEW

Within the Mark Twain National Forest, hundreds of miles of trail await the adventurer. These include steep creek drainages, plateaus and large sections of the Ozark Trail. (More information on this trail comes later in this book.)

More than 78,000 acres of the MTNF are managed as "semi-primitive areas," where the only access is by mountain bike, by hiking or by horseback. Semi-primitive areas differ from congressionally designated wilderness in that resources, such as timber and wildlife, are deliberately managed.

Several highlights of these "semi-primitive areas" include three National Recreation Trails: the 24-mile Berryman Trail, the 5-mile Crane Lake Trail and the 42-mile Ridge Runner Trail.

The MTNF also manages about 265,000 acres for "semi-primitive *motorized* recreation." These are areas open to ATVs, motocross and offer some challenging single and double track for mountain bikers as well—such as Chadwick, which has more than 125 miles of trails winding in and out of deep forested hollows and along ridge tops.

All seven congressionally designated wilderness areas have great hiking trails, but are closed to MTB'ing. Make sure you take your hiking boots to enjoy these incredible trails.

Besides wilderness and semi-primitive areas, the MTNF also maintains about 26,000 acres as "special areas," managed to protect unusual environmental, cultural and historical resources.

CAMPGROUNDS: There are more than 40 campgrounds and picnic areas in the MTNF. They are usually located near a spring, a stream, lake, towering bluff or other scenic area. Float camps, accessible by water, are available on the Eleven Point River.

Campgrounds and picnic areas vary from one-table sites to developed campgrounds. Some have walks, trails and restrooms that are handicapped-accessible. Camping fees vary, with special fees for group camping or use of pavilions. Some areas also have day-use or parking fees for non-campers.

FLOAT STREAMS: The Forest has more than 350 miles of streams suitable for floating with canoes, kayaks, rafts and inner tubes. Some, such as the St. Francis on the Potosi-Fredericktown Ranger District, have seasonal white water but may be too shallow for floating most of the year.

Favorite float streams are the Eleven Point River, the Current, Big and Little Piney, Gasconade, North Fork, Huzzah, Courtois, Meramec, St. Francis, Black, Beaver, Turkey and the Swan. The Forest Service and the Missouri Department of Conservation maintain river accesses on the most popular streams. Private outfitters are available in most of these areas.

DRIVING TOURS: Most roads through the MTNF are scenic and a few are outstanding. The scenery is amazing from mid-April to early May when redbuds and dogwoods bloom and again in mid-October to early November when the leaves are changing.

The Glade Top Trail (Forest Road 147) is a 17-mile, winding gravel road that takes you through cedar-dotted knobs to the Ava-Cassville Ranger District. The Caney Picnic Area offers vistas of surrounding glades and northern Arkansas mountains.

Skyline Drive on the Eleven Point Ranger District is a four-mile paved loop along a ridge top off of Hwy 103 south of Van Buren. This drive has scenic vistas of surrounding hills and valleys.

Sugar Camp Road also offers ridge-top views of Ozark scenery. This 10-mile forest drive runs between Hwy 112 near Roaring River State Park and Hwy 86 near Eagle Rock.

FISHING: The streams and lakes contain bass, bluegill, sunfish, crappie and catfish. Two of the forest's spring-fed streams—Mill Creek and Spring Creek—have wild rainbow trout.

The Little Piney Creek, the Eleven Point National Scenic River and the North Fork of the White River also have sections stocked with rainbow trout. These areas require Missouri trout stamps in addition to fishing licenses. Lakes range from 10 acres to the 440-acre Council Bluff Lake.

WILDERNESS AREAS: The Mark Twain National Forest includes seven congressionally designated wildernesses: Bell Mountain, Rock Pile Mountain, Irish, Paddy Creek, Hercules Glades, Devil's Backbone and Piney Creek. These wilderness lands, totaling more than 63,000 acres, are natural areas.

Mountain biking is strictly prohibited. Hikers, backpackers and horseback riders, however, can seek them out for peace and solitude. Hunting, fishing and primitive camping are allowed. Trailheads with limited parking spaces are located next to the wildernesses.

WILDLIFE: The forest has 175 species of birds, 50 species of mammals and 70 species of amphibians and reptiles. Wildlife includes whitetail deer, turkey, quail, doves, ducks, geese, rabbits, raccoons, squirrels, opossums, woodchucks, bobcats and coyotes. Hunting, with a valid Missouri license, in season, is permitted.

EQUESTRIAN USE: The MTNF has many areas for horseback riding. Some of these are the Berryman on the Potosi-Fredericktown Ranger District; Cole Creek, Kaintuck and Big Piney on the Houston-Rolla-Cedar Creek Ranger District; the Victory on the Poplar Bluff Ranger District; and the Blue Ridge on the Doniphan-Eleven Point Ranger District. Riders also can use the Ozark Trail's Trace Creek and Between the Rivers sections and most forest roads.

MANAGEMENT CODE: The Mark Twain, as all national forests, is managed for recreation, timber, wilderness, minerals, watershed and habitat for fish and wildlife. The main values of the Mark Twain National Forest focus on ecology, aesthetics, wildlife and recreation, in that order.

MARK TWAIN NATIONAL FOREST DISTRICT RANGER STATIONS

AVA–CASSVILLE– WILLOW SPRINGS RANGER DISTRICT

Ava Office
1103 South Jefferson
P.O. Box 188
Ava, MO 65608
(417) 683-4428

Cassville Office
Highway 248 East
P.O. Box 310
Cassville, MO 65625
(417) 847-2144

Willow Springs Office
Old Springfield Road
P.O. Box 99
Willow Springs, MO 65793
(417) 469-3155

DONIPHAN– ELEVEN POINT RANGER DISTRICT

Doniphan Office
1104 Walnut
Doniphan, MO 63935
(573) 996-2153

Winona Office
Highway 19 North
Route 1 Box 1908
Winona, MO 65588
(573) 325-4233

Van Buren Office
Watercress Road
P.O. Box 69
Van Buren, MO 63965
(573) 323-4216

SALEM RANGER DISTRICT

1301 South Main, Hwy 195
P.O. Box 460
Salem, MO 65560
(573) 729-6656

POTOSI– FREDERICKTOWN RANGER DISTRICT

Potosi Office, Hwy 8 West
P.O. Box 188
Potosi, MO 63664
(573) 438-5427

Fredericktown Office
1051 Madison 212
Fredericktown, MO 63645
(573) 783-7225

HOUSTON–ROLLA– CEDAR CREEK RANGER DISTRICT

Houston Office
108 S. Sam Houston Blvd.
Houston, MO 65483
(417) 967-4194

Rolla Office
401 Fairgrounds Road
Houston, MO 65401
(573) 364-4621

Cedar Creek Office
4549 State Road H
Fulton, MO 65251
(573) 592-1400

POPLAR BLUFF RANGER DISTRICT

1420 Maud St.
P.O. Box 988
Poplar Bluff, MO 63901
(573) 785-1475

Did You Know . . .

Timber production in the MTNF in 1990 was approximately 58.3 million board feet, approximately 11.4 percent of the total in Missouri.

The Viburnum Trend, the premier area for U.S. lead mining and milling, is located mostly within the MTNF.

It produces about 90 percent of the nation's annual lead ore.

More than 50 percent of annual production comes from federally owned mines within the forest.

SIDE TRIP:

GLADE TOP TRAIL

When you're ready to take a break from mountain biking, but not from the scenery, check out the Glade Top Trail—one of only three National Scenic Byways in Missouri. This 23-mile gravel road (FR 147) weaves through narrow ridge tops above the surrounding countryside. Travelers are treated to numerous views from the Springfield Plateau to the north and the St. Francis and Boston Mountains to the south.

The drive is accessible from Ava by taking Hwy 5 south to Hwy A and Douglas County Road A-409. From the south, take Hwy 95 just north of Longrun, or from Hwy 125 about four miles north of the intersection with U.S. Hwy 160.

The trail has hardly changed since CCC workers built the two-lane gravel road in the late 1930s. Local residents have long celebrated the brilliant red/orange fall foliage of the area by sponsoring the "Flaming Fall Revue" each year in mid-October, with a barbecue and music festival.

A Spring Flowering Tour is also sponsored annually. This tour highlights the dogwood, serviceberry, redbud and wild fruit trees along the National Forest Scenic Byway.

Year-round, abundant wildlife such as white-tailed deer, wild turkey, quail, squirrels, rabbits and numerous songbirds are prevalent within this part of the forest. The glades are also home for wildlife not often encountered in the Ozarks, such as the roadrunner, collared lizard, pygmy rattlesnake, scorpion and the Bachman's Sparrow—an endangered species.

Look for the following points of interest: Hayden Bald State Natural Area, at the north end; The Three Sisters—a trio of limestone bald knobs; Watershed Divide—where water flows east into the Little Northfork River and west into Beaver Creek; Caney Lookout Tower; The Pinnacle, an old, unsuccessful gold mine; and the Caney Picnic Area, site of the "Flaming Fall Revue."

LEGEND

(1) **ST. LOUIS & EASTERN REGION**

(2) **COLUMBIA & CENTRAL REGION**

(3) **KANSAS CITY & WESTERN REGION**

(4) **SPRINGFIELD & OZARK MOUNTAINS REGION**

(5) **ROLLA & OZARK HIGHLANDS REGION**

(6) **OZARK TRAIL**

(7) **SOUTHEAST REGION**

© *Cartographic Works 1998*

QUICK REFERENCE TABLE OF CONTENTS

REFER TO PAGES 6 - 9 FOR A COMPLETE LIST OF TRAILS

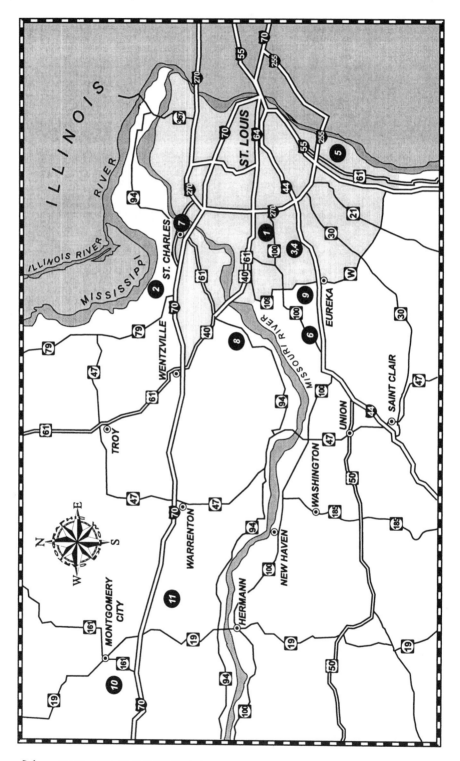

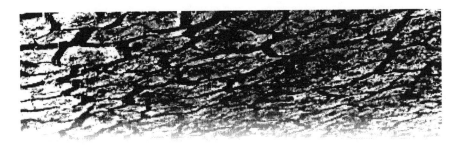

ST. LOUIS &
EASTERN REGION TRAILS

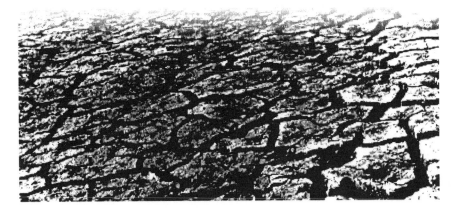

ST. LOUIS & EASTERN REGION

1. QUEENY PARK

BIKE TRAIL & EQUESTRIAN TRAILS

NEAREST TOWN: Ballwin (St. Louis County).

DIRECTIONS: Queeny Park is a county park located west on Manchester Road off of I-270, then right on Weidmann Road.

TRAIL DESCRIPTION: The main trail system at Queeny Park is used heavily by walkers, runners, cyclists and equestrians.

HIGHLIGHTS: The Missouri State Cyclo-cross Championships are held here every November.

HAZARDS: There are a lot of dogs walking their owners here.

AREA INFORMATION: A rare urban location for "legalized" mountain biking.

This 569-acre park has 7.8 miles of MTB trails, 1.5 miles of which are paved. Back in the hilly, wooded sections of the park there are additional miles of horse trails with some jumps. These are also open to mountain biking.

This park provides habitat for eagles, hawks, songbirds, turkey, doves, quail, shorebirds, herons and waterfowl. Deer, rabbits and squirrels also abound. Bluegill, carp, catfish and crappie are plentiful.

ADDITIONAL THOUGHTS: The Dog Museum is on the other side of the park, at the Mason Road entrance: (314) 821-3647.

CONTACT INFO: Queeny Park: (636) 391-0900 or 391-0922. St. Louis County Parks Department, 550 Weidmann Road, Ballwin, MO 63011. (314) 889-2863.

DISTANCE: Bike trail: 7.8 miles, 1.5 of which is paved. The horse and mountain bike trail is a 20-mile loop.

TERRAIN: Part of this trail is paved and gravel roads. The dirt trail section is moderately difficult.

RIDING TIME: 2 - 4 hours.

LAND STATUS: St. Louis County Park.

SERVICES & ACTIVITIES: Restroom and parking lot. Fishing, hiking and mountain biking are permitted. Camping is not. Seasonal indoor ice rink and outdoor roller hockey rink.

TRAILHEAD: Follow the signs. Stop in the Rec Complex building to look at their trails map.

RATING: Great for beginning riders.

38 — SHOW ME MOUNTAIN BIKING

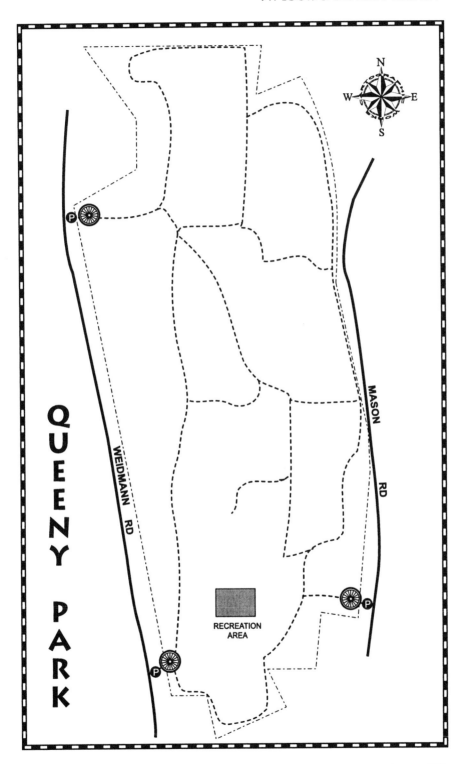

QUEENY PARK

WEIDMANN RD

MASON RD

RECREATION
AREA

2. AUGUST A. BUSCH MEMORIAL CONSERVATION AREA

BUSCH HIKING & BIKING TRAIL

NEAREST TOWN: Weldon Spring (St. Charles County).
DIRECTIONS: Hwy 40/61 to Hwy 94 south, 1.5 miles on Hwy D.
TRAIL DESCRIPTION: The Busch Hiking & Biking Trail, a 3.2-mile hard-gravel loop, begins off of Road B within the area. It passes over a dam on Lake 19 and passes agricultural fields. It does cross several roads open to vehicles. There are also six other hiking-only trails throughout the park, which total 5.3 miles. Watch for signs. This is a scenic ride. If you're looking for hair-raising off-road trails, you'll want to continue on to Weldon Spring's Lost Valley trail.
HIGHLIGHTS: There are great maps and interpretive signs peppered throughout the park and it's staffed by a well-educated crew of naturalists should you have any questions at all.
AREA INFORMATION: This 6,987-acre area has 32 lakes, hiking trails, a firing range and fishing. Before World War II, this area was populated with farms and small towns. More than 30 cemeteries stand as testimony to the pioneer families of the early 1800s. The oldest tombstone here dates to 1817. In 1941, the U.S. government bought more than 17,000 acres to manufacture and store explosives. One hundred bunkers were built to store TNT. The Missouri Department of Conservation bought 7,000 acres from the government in 1947, and Mrs. August Busch made a donation in memory of her husband. Most of the bunkers are now empty and are welded shut.

Oak and hickory woodlands and Indian grasses are prevalent here. Switchgrass and bluestem are present in smaller quantities. Many of the birds you will spot here during the spring and late summer to early fall are migratory birds, such as plovers and sandpipers, looking for insects along the shores.

ADDITIONAL THOUGHTS: This is a great Sunday afternoon leisurely ride. If you are looking for an easy ride while you're just getting into mountain biking or if you just want to see some new scenery, this is the place.
CONTACT INFO: A. Busch Memorial Conservation Area, 2360 Hwy D, St. Charles, MO 63304. (636) 441-4554 or (636) 441-4669.
DISTANCE: 3.2 miles.
TERRAIN: Hard gravel.
RIDING TIME: One hour.
LAND STATUS: Department of Conservation.
SERVICES & ACTIVITIES: Fishing, hiking, restrooms, picnic area, information and interpretive center, nature viewing blinds, auto tour and boat rental. Family fishing fair each June. Lake 33 is the largest lake here, with 182 fishable acres. It is stocked with largemouth bass, bluegill, crappie and catfish.
TRAILHEAD: Accessible from Road B, within the area.
RATING: Easy.

Ride the easy bike trail, walk one of the many foot paths, and bring a book to read or fish at one of the numerous lakes.

3. CASTLEWOOD STATE PARK

GROTPETER, LONE WOLF, RIVER SCENE, & STINGING NETTLE TRAILS

NEAREST TOWN: St. Louis (St. Louis County).
DIRECTIONS: Castlewood is outside St. Louis near Ballwin, along Keifer Creek Road. Take Hwy 340 south until it turns into Keifer Creek Road. Go east on Kiefer Creek Road, off New Ballwin Road from Hwy 100. Or, from St. Louis, take I-270 to Manchester west and turn south on Ries Road. Turn left on Keifer Creek Road and follow it to the trailhead. If you are coming from I-44, exit at Hwy 141, Meramec Station Road, go right (north). Turn left onto Big Bend. Big Bend turns into Oak Street. Turn left at Ries Road. Go over the hill and turn left at the Castlewood sign.
TRAIL DESCRIPTION: The three-mile Grotpeter Trail is hilly and technical as it winds through the park's wooded uplands. It can be accessed near the first picnic shelter. A one-mile hike is also possible from this trail.

River Scene Trail is a 1.5-mile loop that begins opposite the entrance road to the first picnic shelter. It ascends to the bluffs along the Meramec River, then goes down to the floodplain along the river's edge and back to the starting point. The River Scene Trail is mostly dirt, fairly flat, with several short, technical sections.

The Stinging Nettle Trail, named after the plant that lines the trail, is three miles long, primarily flat with several hills. A new trail called the Lone Wolf Trail just recently opened.

The Chubb trail also passes through Castlewood State Park, but it is south of the river and is not accessible from this trail.

HIGHLIGHTS: A fun sprint with a great view along the river. Multiple loop, mostly flat and easy riding, with interesting sights.

HAZARDS: Remember to keep an eye out for horseback riders, a lot of walkers and hikers. Also, in spring, the rising river often reaches beyond its banks, leaving the lowland trail under water or at the very least pure muck for weeks at a time. Please avoid the trail when muddy, since heavy use at these times can cause a real problem.

AREA INFORMATION: This large, heavily wooded park is a mountain-biking must-see. The Meramec River flows through the park, making it popular for canoeing and fishing as well.

An integral part of Castlewood's past are the majestic white limestone bluffs that tower above the Meramec. The stately wooded bluffs are reminiscent of the turreted walls of medieval European castles. This gorgeous wilderness has attracted people for centuries. During the early 1900s, Castlewood was a premiere resort. From 1915 until about 1940, St. Louisans flocked by the thousands to the area for weekends of canoeing, dancing and sunning on Lincoln Beach along the river. During its heyday, trains deposited

up to 10,000 weekenders at three small depots located at the foot of the Meramec River bluffs. A grand staircase, which still exists, guided the fun-seekers to the three resort hotels and numerous summer cabins once located in the area.

The 1,779-acre park also contains a wide variety of natural habitats, including forested hills, a small stream valley, flood plain, gravel bars and the Meramec River. A floodplain forest—a rapidly vanishing feature of Missouri's landscape—is preserved here. It includes silver maple, box elder, black willow, white ash and sycamore trees. Slippery elm, white oak, northern red oak, shagbark hickory and redbud cover the uplands. Wildlife include cricket frogs, wild turkey, white-tailed deer, kingfishers and great blue herons.

Initially formed by two separate land acquisitions, Castlewood State Park now straddles both sides of the Meramec River. It is also part of the Meramec River Recreation Area, which stretches 108 river miles from Meramec State Park to the river's confluence with the Mississippi River south of St. Louis. This extended recreation area includes a series of existing and proposed open spaces along the Meramec River that will someday be connected by trails.

ADDITIONAL THOUGHTS: This is true off-road single track. Be prepared for anything: dirt, sand, rocks—even mud. Remember, too, that this is an urban trail that sees a lot of use, so leave the bonzai-type riding for the Surge cola commercials.

CONTACT INFO: Castlewood State Park, 152 Keifer Creek Rd. Ballwin, MO 63021. (636) 527-6481. St. Louis County Park info: (314) 889-2863. Open dawn to dusk.

DISTANCE: Bluffs Trail: 0.6 mile, River Scene Trail: 3 miles, Grotpeter Trail: 3 miles.

TERRAIN: Varies from bottomland riding (basically flat) to steep hill climbs along creek valley and ridge to ridge riding. Hilly and technical on the Grotpeter Trail.

RIDING TIME: 2 hours.

LAND STATUS: Department of Natural Resources.

SERVICES & ACTIVITIES: Hiking, fishing and boating. No camping allowed. River ramp at east edge of the park north of the Meramec River. Fishermen can enjoy angling for bluegill, smallmouth bass and catfish. Forty picnic sites and two shelters are also located here. The park has water and restrooms.

TRAILHEAD: After crossing the bridge, the trailhead is on the right, near the gazebo.

RATING: Easy to difficult. Something for everyone.

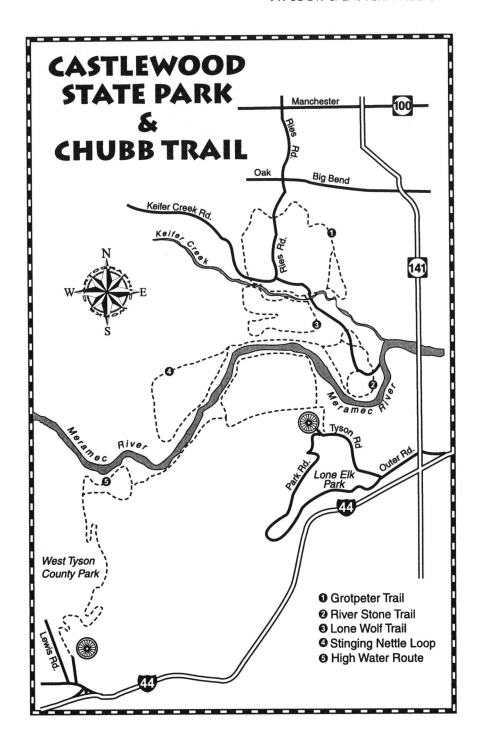

CASTLEWOOD STATE PARK & CHUBB TRAIL

Manchester

100

Ries Rd.

Oak   Big Bend

Keifer Creek Rd.

Keifer Creek

Ries Rd.

141

❶

N
W   E
S

❸

❹

❷

Meramec River

Tyson Rd.

Meramec   River

Park Rd.

Outer Rd.

❺

Lone Elk Park

44

West Tyson County Park

Lewis Rd.

44

❶ Grotpeter Trail
❷ River Stone Trail
❸ Lone Wolf Trail
❹ Stinging Nettle Loop
❺ High Water Route

Dirt gypsy Margo Carroll. Photo by Peggy Welch.

NOTES:

_____

_____

_____

_____

_____

_____

_____

_____

4. WEST TYSON COUNTY PARK

CHUBB TRAIL

NEAREST TOWN: St. Louis (St. Louis County).
DIRECTIONS: From St. Louis, go west on I-44. Get off at Lewis Road Exit 265. Enter West Tyson Park, go up the hill to the end of the road and park. Or, the other end of Chubb Trail can be reached by exiting I-44 at Meramec Road (Hwy 141). Turn right (west) on the Outer Road. Follow this to Lone Elk County Park. The Chubb Trailhead is the fire road before the Lone Elk gates.
TRAIL DESCRIPTION: The Chubb is the most challenging trail in the St. Louis area. It is a seven-mile dirt and gravel trail between West Tyson County Park and Lone Elk Park (14 miles round-trip). It has very challenging hills and some very fast stretches. Terrain is rocky and usually slippery. There are some truly nasty drop-offs. After those tough climbs you are often rewarded with great views.

The first four miles, starting at the Tyson Trailhead, are primarily steep climbs and descents. The middle three miles are flat, following the river bank (very much like Stinging Nettle Trail at Castlewood). A mile or so of uphill fire roads brings you to Lone Elk Park at the other end.

The seven-mile trail was developed by St. Louis County Department of Parks and Recreation and the Missouri Department of Natural Resources through the cooperative effort of the Meramec River Recreation Association, which is creating a 108-mile natural corridor along the Meramec by joining together parks and trails.

HIGHLIGHTS: Popular, long descents.

HAZARDS: Definitely wear a helmet on this ride.

AREA INFORMATION: Lone Elk Park has bison and elk, picnicking, a lake and more. The Tyson end has camping and picnic tables.

ADDITIONAL THOUGHTS: Less extreme riders like to start at the Lone Elk end, which allows you to warm up some. Great views from this trail. From the West Tyson end, you'll find a good mix of very tough technical stuff with fast stretches. As one biker put it, "The Tyson end of the trail eats bikes."

I have heard of more major mechanical problems on this trail than anywhere else (a good friend of mine broke his carbon fiber Cadex in half). Make sure you and your bike are ready before riding here. The river is prone to flooding, putting some of the trail under water. This trail also goes through Castlewood State Park.

CONTACT INFO: St. Louis County Parks: (314) 889-2863.

DISTANCE: 7 miles. 14 miles round-trip.

TERRAIN: Everything from good to bad to ugly.

RIDING TIME: 2 - 3 hours round-trip to all day.

LAND STATUS: County Park.

SERVICES & ACTIVITIES: Water and campsites at the West Tyson end of the trail. Call for camping reservations. Nearby, St. Louis has every service you might need.

TRAILHEAD: Trailheads are to the right of the entrance to Lone Elk Park, and the fire road at the West Tyson parking lot.

RATING: Moderate to difficult.

5. CLIFF CAVE COUNTY PARK

NEAREST TOWN: St. Louis (St. Louis County).
DIRECTIONS: Take 270 south (south of I-44), cross over I-55, where it changes to Hwy 255, take Telegraph Road Exit (last exit before crossing the river into Illinois). Turn right off ramp, head south on Telegraph to Cliff Cave Road. Turn left. Follow Cliff Cave Road through a neighborhood and then it goes right into the park.
TRAIL DESCRIPTION: This heavily wooded 222-acre park has a loop MTB trail that goes alongside and up over the top of the cave. Stop at the first parking lot for access to the trail.
HIGHLIGHTS: Check out the mouth of the cave.
HAZARDS: Cover your legs during the summer months. Poison ivy is very bad here. Don't forget to wash off with soap thoroughly after your ride. Remember, poison ivy oils can be easily transmitted by your hands from shoelaces to your face, if you rub your eyes or something, so wash your hands thoroughly after your ride.
AREA INFORMATION: This river-bottom park occasionally floods with the spring rise of the Mississippi River. Great view of the river from the hills.
ADDITIONAL THOUGHTS: Caving is by permit only.
CONTACT INFO: St. Louis County Park: (314) 889-2863. Call Ranger Keith Goldecker at (314) 963-9211 for more information.
DISTANCE: Numerous trails, more are being blazed. At present, at least 2 miles of trail.
TERRAIN: Hard packed and rock. Mostly dirt and gravel, crosses tree roots. Pretty tough.
RIDING TIME: 1 - 3 hours.
LAND STATUS: St. Louis County Park.
SERVICES & ACTIVITIES: Fishing, picnic tables, restrooms, shelter. No water, electric or playgrounds.
TRAILHEAD: Park at first parking area.
RATING: Easy to moderate.

Angel Black enjoying fall's display
at Cliff Cave County Park in St. Louis County.

6. GREENSFELDER COUNTY PARK

DECLUE & DOGWOOD TRAILS

NEAREST TOWN: Eureka (St. Louis County).
DIRECTIONS: From St. Louis go west on I-44. Get off at the Allenton-Six Flags exit. Go north past Six Flags on Allenton Road for two miles, enter the park. Near the Visitors Center, park in the gravel parking lot on the left.
TRAIL DESCRIPTION: This is one of the toughest places to ride in Missouri. Unlike nearby Six Flags Amusement Park, this here trail is a natural roller coaster with no admission charge and no $8 cheese sandwiches. There's a series of 25 miles of very challenging trails. Be prepared for technical single track, steep climbs and descents over big rocks and roots. Not much fun when it's muddy.

Only DeClue and Dogwood Trails are open for MTB'ing. The rest are only open to equestrians and hiking and are clearly marked. These regulations are enforced by the park rangers and the equestrians. A new MTB trail is being built for spring 1999.

HIGHLIGHTS: Scary, steep downhills with good-sized drop-offs. Sometimes you can hear the roller coaster at Six Flags on parts of the trail. This is a good choice if you're looking for solitude, since not too many riders come here.

HAZARDS: Not paying enough attention to the changing terrain. There's enough ticks here to make a hound dog never leave the porch again.

AREA INFORMATION: This area was once owned by local environmentalist and open space supporter A. P. Greensfelder. This park has 1,758 acres of oak and hickory forest. In addition to mountain bike trails, it has hiking trails, a nature learning center, camping and more. Nearby, in Gray Summit, be sure and visit the Shaw Arboretum (no MTB'ing allowed). The arboretum has hiking trails,

a gorgeous wetland area with observation blind and extensive prairies and other walking trails. Nearby Purina Farms makes for a great tour as well.

ADDITIONAL THOUGHTS: There are other trails in the park that prohibit bikers—try not to get on the wrong ones. This is a heavily used equestrian area.

CONTACT INFO: St. Louis County Parks at (314) 889-2863.

DISTANCE: 4-mile system.

TERRAIN: Hard pack with several rocky sections.

RIDING TIME: Varies from two hours to all afternoon.

LAND STATUS: St. Louis County Parks.

SERVICES & ACTIVITIES: The park has water, restrooms and camping. St. Louis is close by.

TRAILHEAD: Dogwood Shelter.

RATING: Moderate to challenging.

Fall is Jenny Kulier's favorite time to ride Missouri's trails.

7. KATY TRAIL STATE PARK

ST. CHARLES TRAILHEAD

NEAREST TOWN: St. Charles (St. Charles County).

DIRECTIONS: The Katy Trail is accessible from dozens of points along its route. St. Charles is the eastern-most trailhead, accessible from I-70. Take the St. Charles 5th Street Exit. Go north. Turn right onto Boonslick Road. Take Boonslick Road to Riverfront Drive and park. See map for more information. The trail follows Hwy 94 along the Missouri River and currently ends in Sedalia.

TRAIL DESCRIPTION: The Katy Trail is the longest rails-to-trails conversion in the country. This is a flat bike trail as opposed to the more aggressive rides highlighted throughout this book. Grades never exceed five percent. The trail is open to hikers and bikers and is wheelchair accessible.

If you're looking for a long distance cardio workout or just a great easy ride, the Katy Trail is a great trail to explore. The hard-packed, eight-foot-wide trail offers many great views of the scenery along the Missouri River. It also passes through many historic, small communities in the river bottoms.

HIGHLIGHTS: Great stretches of solitude. Gorgeous bluffs and river views.

HAZARDS: The edges of the trail tend to get soft with heavy rainfall. Bring your Skin-So-Soft or insect repellent.

AREA INFORMATION: Call the Greater St. Charles Convention and Visitors Bureau at 1 (800) 366-2427. They've got a series of free eco-tourism brochures on everything from birdwatching, to hiking and biking, to wildflower and fall leaf tours.

ADDITIONAL THOUGHTS: The trail will extend on east to Machens perhaps as soon as spring 1999. If you're looking for camping, there's a campground in St. Charles called Sundermeier RV Park, 1 (800) 929-0832, that has great hot showers and is a good base camp if you plan on spending several days in this area.

CONTACT INFO: Missouri Department of Natural Resources Information Hotline: 1 (800) 334-6946.

DISTANCE: 185 miles.

TERRAIN: Hard-packed chat surface. Pedals almost like pavement except on soft shoulders and after weeks of soaking rains.

I've seen mountain bikes, hybrids and road bikes all fare equally well on the trail.

RIDING TIME: A few hours for a leisurely visit. Three to five days to explore the whole length of the 200-mile trail. I've heard of several athletes doing the whole trail in two days but what's the rush?

LAND STATUS: Department of Natural Resources

SERVICES & ACTIVITIES: Restrooms, bike repair and rental, food and lodging. Camping is allowed in designated areas only.

Many service locations are available all along the trail, separated by distances between five and 30 miles, making this a great training ride for even the most caffeine dependent bikers (did I hear someone say mocha?). Trailside services in St. Charles are as complete as it gets. They range from luxurious bed and breakfasts and restaurants to cafes and the Touring Cyclist Bike Shop, right on Main Street.

TRAILHEAD: St. Charles, Greens Bottom Road, Weldon Spring Conservation Area, Defiance, Matson, Augusta, etc. Check out DNR's free Katy Trail maps: 1 (800) 334-6946. Or order *The Complete Katy Trail Guidebook* ($14.95) from Pebble Publishing 1 (800) 576-7322. It has everything from mileage charts, a pull-out map, services, histories of the towns, listing of all B&Bs, you name it.

RATING: Easy. Flat, smooth gravel trail makes for a leisurely and scenic ride.

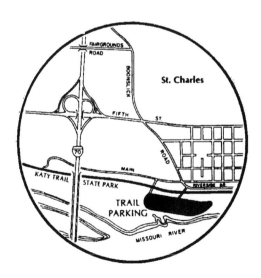

Margo Carroll pedals alongside a field of spring wildflowers.

8. WELDON SPRING CONSERVATION AREA

LOST VALLEY TRAIL

NEAREST TOWN: Weldon Spring (southwest St. Charles County).
DIRECTIONS: Take Hwy 94 south past Hwy 40/64 about 5 miles. Just before the one-lane bridge, slow down and turn right into the large gravel parking lot, just before the Little Femme Osage Creek.
TRAIL DESCRIPTION: Eight-mile loop. The first three miles are mainly flat double and single track. There's a short climb followed by a downhill and rolling hills. Half of the trail is a flat wide country road closed to auto traffic, the second half winds through forest and meadows and along ridges and many streams.
HIGHLIGHTS: The wildflowers are awesome! Spring rides are highly recommended. Pink and purple phlox, may apples and bluets dot the green landscape. Spring also brings many nesting great blue herons, noted for their slender profiles and wide wingspans.
HAZARDS: This area is popular during hunting season. (Call the Conservation Department to find out when.)

AREA INFORMATION: The total contiguous acreage of Weldon Spring, Howell Island and the Busch Conservation Area is 16,918 acres, 7,356 of which comprise Weldon Spring. The area was named for John Weldon, who received a Spanish land grant in 1796 for 425 acres. Nearly 150 years later, during World War II, the government acquired 17,000 acres here for the construction of a munitions plant. It was then owned by the University of Missouri and in 1978, the Conservation Department acquired this property. Along the road, you'll notice a fine chert trail that looks like the Katy Trail, except that it has WARNING signs posted on all sides. The government is cleaning up the old munitions plant where atom-bomb research was done during World War II. This area is like the cousin St. Louis doesn't want to talk about.

ADDITIONAL THOUGHTS: This is a great, forested ride for fall and hot summer days when you need shade. Carry a map or a GPS. It's easy to miss turns, especially after the big downhill.

Peggy Welch enjoys a moment of reflection at Weldon Spring Conservation Area.

CONTACT INFO: Weldon Spring Conservation Area, (636) 441-4554.
DISTANCE: 8-mile loop.
TERRAIN: This trail gives you a wide variety of terrain from hard-packed dirt to gravel. After you get over the biggest hill, it's all downhill. You can easily hit some speed here.
RIDING TIME: 1 - 3 hours.
LAND STATUS: Missouri Department of Conservation.
SERVICES & ACTIVITIES: Water at Busch on Hwy 94, 2 miles away; St. Louis nearby.
RATING: Easy to moderate. Great for beginners and intermediates.

9. ROCKWOODS RANGE CONSERVATION AREA

EQUESTRIAN TRAIL

NEAREST TOWN: Eureka (St. Louis County).

DIRECTIONS: From Eureka, take I-44 west for 3 miles to Allenton Road (Exit 261). Go north and turn west on the outer road (Fox Creek Road). Follow Fox Creek Road for 1.25 miles to the parking lot on the right. Continue on Fox Creek Road for 2.25 miles to access another trailhead parking lot on the right.

TRAIL DESCRIPTION: There are two trails here open to MTB'ers. From the first trailhead access off of Fox Creek Road, you can access the Fox Creek Spur Trail. About a half mile into this ride, if you take the right fork, you will be on the approximately three-mile Round House Loop Trail, which skirts a drainage.

If you decide to stick to the Fox Creek Spur Trail, continue left (or straight) on the Fox Creek Trail to avoid riding the Round House Loop Trail. If you stick left, you will cross the Greenrock Hiking Trail, a drainage and several scenic rest areas before ending up at the other trail access 2.25 miles further down Fox Creek Road. This is not a loop trail.

At the northern end of the Round House loop, you can double back and ride back to your car, by turning left onto Fox Run Trail. Or, you can go even farther into this 1,388-acre conservation area, by going right on the Fox Run Trail instead of left, which takes you to the other trail access 2.25 miles further down Fox Creek Road.

HIGHLIGHTS: This area is 90 percent forested. There are a couple of benches at overlooks.

HAZARDS: Remember that you are sharing this trail with horses— so always give right-of-way.

AREA INFORMATION: This 1,388 acres area is sandwiched in between Allenton and Hencken Roads to the east and Fox Creek Road to the west and south. If you have to bail from the trail, take any of these roads south. You will either come upon the trailhead, or if you end up at I-44, go west on Fox Creek Road for 1.25 miles to the trailhead parking lot.

ADDITIONAL THOUGHTS: Bicycles are permitted only on roads and trails open to vehicular traffic and horseback riding and on service roads posted closed to motorized vehicles, except when further restricted by posting.
CONTACT INFO: Missouri Department of Conservation St. Louis Region Rockwoods Conservation Area Office: (636) 458-2236.
DISTANCE: 8.5 miles of trail.
TERRAIN: Limestone base, rolling hills, flat ridge rides, going up and down hills. Not real steep. Mostly barrier free except for the occasional tree. This trail can all be ridden, without any portages or extremely steep sections.
RIDING TIME: 2 hours.
LAND STATUS: Missouri Department of Conservation.
SERVICES & ACTIVITIES: No water, camping or restrooms. Greensfelder County Park is nearby.
TRAILHEAD: Two parking lots on Fox Creek Road.
RATING: Easy to moderate.

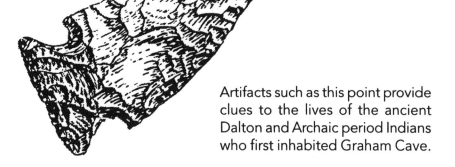

Artifacts such as this point provide clues to the lives of the ancient Dalton and Archaic period Indians who first inhabited Graham Cave.

10. GRAHAM CAVE STATE PARK

LOUTRE RIVER & INDIAN GLADE TRAILS

NEAREST TOWN: Danville (Montgomery County).

DIRECTIONS: Take the Danville Exit (Exit 170) north off I-70, then take Hwy TT and follow the signs.

TRAIL DESCRIPTION: The park, which borders the Loutre River, has two multi-use trails, being shared by hikers and mountain bikers. The Loutre River Trail is a two-mile loop. The Indian Glade Trail (west of the entrance road) is a one-mile bike ride (one way).

HIGHLIGHTS: Special features include glades, savannas and sandstone bluffs with overhangs and wet-season waterfalls and creeks.

HAZARDS: There are several rocky trail sections.

AREA INFORMATION: Graham Cave, a site of very early human occupation, is the principal feature of the 357-acre state park. During the 1950s, archaeological finds from the sheltered cave proved that Missouri was inhabited by Native Americans thousands of years earlier than previously believed. Evidence of Indian habitation extended six feet into the floor of the cave and were radiocarbon dated to be at least 10,000 years old.

Archaeologists from the University of Missouri have uncovered artifacts that provide clues to the lifestyle of the ancient Dalton and Archaic period Indians who first inhabited the cave. These early Indians lived in Graham Cave before the development of burial mounds, pottery or even agriculture. They depended mainly on hunting and fishing for food. These people were spear throwers, not bow and arrow hunters. They occupied the cave seasonally and apparently believed in the supernatural.

Pieces of pottery found in the cave indicated that it was occupied by a more recent culture of Indians. Archaeologists believe that a long time lapse separated abandonment of the cave by the Dalton and Archaic period peoples and its use by pottery makers.

Graham Cave is named after the first settler who owned the cave property in 1816. Dr. Robert Graham bought the site from the son of Daniel Boone. Between 1829 and 1850, the last human inhabitant of the cave, a French-Indian, built a log cabin in the cave's entrance before moving elsewhere. Later, farm animals were sheltered in the "natural barn."

Today the cave is fenced off since the 100-foot-long expanse has not yet been fully excavated but inside the entrance to the cave, interpretive signs point out interesting discoveries. The trail to the cave is paved, making this stop particularly accessible.

ADDITIONAL THOUGHTS: There is camping at this park or if you don't want to hear the highway all night, head down Hwy 19 to Hermann to visit the wineries (to ensure a good night's rest) then camp at the Hermann City Park, (573) 486-5308 or 486-5400. It is located at the junction of Hwys 19 & 100 and Gasconade Street.

CONTACT INFO: Graham Cave State Park, Montgomery City, MO 63361. (573) 564-3476 or call 1 (800) 334-6946.

DISTANCE: 3 miles.

TERRAIN: Hilly.

RIDING TIME: An hour. Leave time to explore the cave and the nearby creek beds.

LAND STATUS: Department of Natural Resources.

SERVICES & ACTIVITIES: There are 38 basic campsites and 15 improved campsites scattered through the woods. Campsites are available year-round on a first-come, first-served basis. The camping area has a modern restroom and hot showers. There are also picnic sites, a shelter and a playground. There's also a boat ramp on the Loutre River.

TRAILHEAD: Follow the trail signs.

RATING: Easy to moderate.

11. DANIEL BOONE CONSERVATION AREA

EQUESTRIAN TRAIL

NEAREST TOWN: Big Spring (Warren County).

DIRECTIONS: From Warrenton, take I-70 west for 11 miles. Go south on Route Y for 3 miles to the area sign, go south on the gravel Tower Road for 2 miles to the horse trail parking lot.

TRAIL DESCRIPTION: Although primarily an equestrian trail, cyclists may use the same trails always giving right-of-way to horses.

In 1943, former Conservation Commissioner A. P. Greensfelder donated the original acreage for this area. Later acquisitions brought this tract to a total of 3,520 acres. This area is primarily an oak and hickory upland forest. The horse trails, which are open to mountain biking, are only open seasonally, from the end of the spring firearms turkey season to the beginning of the fall firearms turkey season. The trail crosses Tower Road several times in case you need to bail from the trail.

HIGHLIGHTS: This trail passes up and down several drainages and traverses near several lakes and ponds.

HAZARDS: Open from end of spring turkey season to beginning of fall turkey season. Wear hunter's orange. Call ahead to make sure that you are only riding it during the time that it is open.

ADDITIONAL THOUGHTS: The Katy Trail State Park is located nearby. To get there, head south on Tower Road to get to Hwy 94 and the Katy Trail. In Daniel Boone Conservation Area, bicycles are permitted only on roads and trails open to vehicular traffic and horseback riding and on service roads posted closed to motorized vehicles, except when further restricted by posting.

CONTACT INFO: Missouri Department of Conservation Central Region Warrenton Office: (636) 456-3368.
DISTANCE: 10 miles, comprised of a shorter western loop and an eastern loop.
TERRAIN: Although the entire ride changes only 300 feet in elevation, there are several technical sections that even challenge horseback riders.
RIDING TIME: 3 hours.
LAND STATUS: Missouri Department of Conservation.
SERVICES & ACTIVITIES: Primitive camping is allowed. No restroom facilities provided.
RATING: Moderate to difficult with several technical sections.

NOTES:

_____

_____

_____

_____

_____

_____

_____

_____

... ROBERTSVILLE STATE PARK

VOLUNTEERS WANTED TO BUILD NEW MTB TRAIL

NEAREST TOWN: Gray Summit (Franklin County).
DIRECTIONS: Less than an hour from St. Louis on I-44 south to Exit NN. Follow the signs to Robertsville State Park 6 miles away on Hwy M.
TRAIL DESCRIPTION: CURRENTLY THERE ARE NO MTB TRAILS AT ROBERTSVILLE STATE PARK, despite the notices posted in several publications. A trail is flagged and is under construction but it isn't completed yet.

The Roberstville Park Association is, however, *interested* in having MTB trails. But they need volunteers to make it happen. Two volunteers have been cutting on a new seven-mile multiple-use loop trail in the park, but this remains more of a dream than a reality.

The park's previous calls for volunteer assistance have gone unanswered, but hopefully a few eyeballs reading this will volunteer to work on this trail. Perhaps in future editions of this book there will be MTB trails in Robertsville for bikers to enjoy from around Missouri and the United States.

The Spice Bush Trail, at 2 miles, and the Roberts Family Cemetery trail, at 0.8 miles, are only open to hikers.
HIGHLIGHTS: Current hiking trails have bluff overlooks, pass through riverside forest and a historic resort site.
AREA INFORMATION: For more outdoor adventures, head south on I-44 for 20 minutes to Meramec State Park.
CONTACT INFO: Park Superintendent, P.O. Box 186, Robertsville, MO 63072. (636) 257-3788.
DISTANCE: Proposed trail would be a 7-mile loop.
TERRAIN: Rolling hills.
SERVICES & ACTIVITIES: Hiking, tent and RV camping.

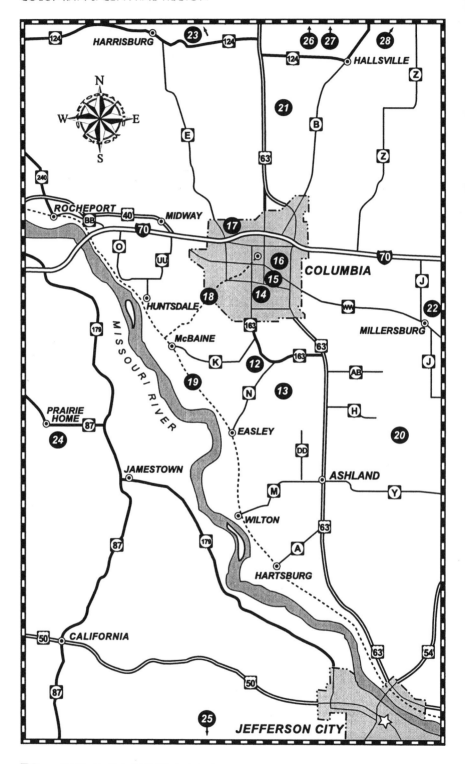

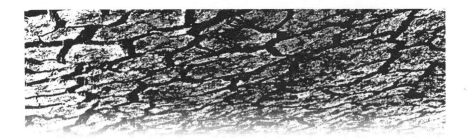

COLUMBIA & CENTRAL REGION TRAILS

COLUMBIA & CENTRAL REGION

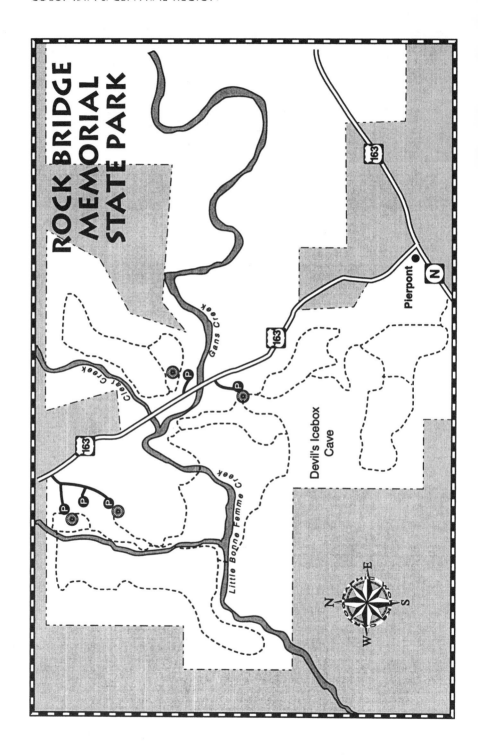

Rob Cline explores the Rock Bridge. Photo by Brett Dufur.

12. ROCK BRIDGE MEMORIAL STATE PARK

VARIOUS TRAILS

NEAREST TOWN: Columbia (Boone County).

DIRECTIONS: Rock Bridge Memorial State Park is just south of Columbia. From I-70, take Hwy 63 south of Columbia for about 8 miles. Turn west on Hwy 163. At Pierpont, start following the signs for Rock Bridge. Turn into the Devil's Icebox parking area. The trails are at either end of the parking area. Or, from Columbia, take Providence Road south and turn east on Hwy 163 (next to Rock Bridge Elementary School). Follow the signs to Devil's Icebox parking lot.

TRAIL DESCRIPTION: Rock Bridge State Park is the most popular spot for mountain biking around Columbia. The park consists of four good loops from 1.5 to 2.5 miles long which can be ridden in any order. The trails are well maintained with virtually no poison ivy along the trail (a major plus) or deadfall blocking the way. The rides range from open fire roads on grassy plains to wooded single track. The trails are generally not very technical but there are a few tricky sections of single track and some difficult steep rocky ascents.

Rock Bridge has numerous trail loops, all of which are well marked and well developed. Maps are generally available at the trailhead, in the little wood information board. Trails are easy, with few climbs, and no really difficult sections. Suitable for beginners and families. These trails are open to mountain bikes on a trial basis—the trails are closed to mountain bikes when the trail is muddy. Call the park office to make sure the trails are open before you go: (573) 442-2249.

HIGHLIGHTS: A short walk from the parking lot off Hwy 163 will lead to a natural bridge known locally as Rock Bridge. The bridge is the roof of a cave that collapsed. Today it serves as an access to an underground cave system.

A quick walk along the boardwalk will bring you to Devil's Ice-box Cave, which you can peek into. It is nice and cool year-round and a great place to rest on a hot summer day. Only experienced cavers with permits are allowed into the six-mile long cave, which has a half-mile long, deep water crossing at the entrance. Caving trips are led by the park and by MU's Wilderness Adventures. Contact the park office for details.

AREA INFORMATION: In the 1820s, Boone County was a frontier sparsely covered with small farms. The natural rock bridge, set in the wooded valley of Little Bonne Femme Creek, seemed a logical place to build a mill for their grains.

A small dam was built beneath the southern opening of the natural bridge. Water flowing over this dam was used to power a grist mill at the site. A blacksmith shop and a general store were constructed and the rock bridge soon became a gathering place for the country folk in the surrounding area.

In later days, the small quarry served as a stage for plays and political rallies. During the 1830s and 1840s, a paper mill was established. Later, McConathy Rye whiskey was produced in the area until a fire destroyed the distillery in 1889. After the fire, the blacksmith shop and store were moved to a nearby hill and given the name Pierpont, "Rock Bridge" in French.

Rock Bridge became a state park in 1957. Throughout the park, you will notice many sinkholes, cave entrances, streams and small springs, all characteristic of "karst" topography. About 300 million years ago, giant oceans deposited many layers of animal and other organic remains, forming a layer called Burlington Limestone. The karst topography is the result of water, which through the years has dissolved parts of the limestone bedrock forming elongated underground passages. This karst topography is common throughout Missouri, and as early settlers searched for a motto for the state, instead of the "Show Me State," many voted for the "Cave State," since Missouri has more than 5,000 caves.

Nearly the entire eastern half of the park is drained by Gans Creek. A 750-acre tract surrounding the creek has been designated the Gans Creek Wild Area and will remain in its natural, wild state. Gans Creek meanders along its course framed by tall bluffs of Burlington Limestone, which overlook the oak and hickory forested valley below.

The Gans Creek area was farmed at one time, but the forest is now quickly returning. Stands of oak and hickory are now reaching full maturity. Persimmon, a variety of maples and wild cherry round out the forest canopy. Hikers can access the Wild Area from the north by taking Rock Quarry Road to Nifong and heading straight onto Bearfield Road until it dead-ends. MTB'ing is not allowed.

ADDITIONAL THOUGHTS: Remember, if it has rained in the last week, call before you head out to ride to get an update on the current trail conditions: (573) 442-2249. The park is closed to mountain biking when the trails are muddy. Park hours are from dawn to dusk year-round.

CONTACT INFO: Rock Bridge Memorial State Park, Columbia, MO 65201. (573) 449-7402.

DISTANCE: 12-mile system.

TERRAIN: Hilly, primarily non-technical.

RIDING TIME: 2 hours.

LAND STATUS: Department of Natural Resources.

SERVICES & ACTIVITIES: Water is available in a second parking area, a short ride north of the Rock Bridge parking lot. There are 33 picnic sites and a shelter located throughout the park. Camping is not available here. Nearby Columbia has everything from great bike shops and great microbrew to great live performances.

TRAILHEAD: At parking lot.

RATING: Easy to moderate.

13. THREE CREEKS CONSERVATION AREA

THREE CREEKS TRAILS

NEAREST TOWNS: Columbia & Ashland (Boone County).

DIRECTIONS: From Columbia, at the junction of I-70 and Hwy 63, go south on Hwy 63 for 8 miles to the Route AB crossing. Turn west (right) on Deer Park Road, go about 2 miles to Three Creeks Conservation Area. Look for a sign pointing the way on the right just before the junction of Hwy 63 and Deer Park Road. Turn right and go about 2 miles until you see a Conservation Department sign. Turn left (staying on main road). Follow this road until it dead-ends at a small parking area. The trailhead is west of the parking area past the gate. The trail to the east is for hikers only.

TRAIL DESCRIPTION: The hilly terrain leading to the confluence of the Turkey, Bass and Bonne Femme Creeks makes for gorgeous scenery and great mountain biking. There are three loops to this trail with a few down-and-back trails heading off from the main loops. The second loop is a shorter steeper section to the right of

THREE CREEKS CONSERVATION AREA

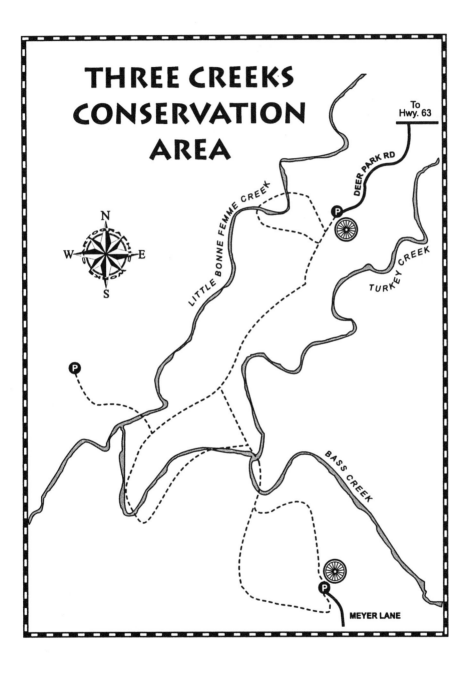

the main trail about a half mile from the parking area. It is more technical than the main loop with lots of deadfall and rocky sections. Each loop has short, flat sections along the banks of the Turkey, Bass and Bonne Femme Creeks. A few of the trails cross the creeks several times.

HIGHLIGHTS: This trail is not too difficult and can be ridden by just about anyone interested in riding short single track. There are bluffs and overlooks that provide great views of the area with everything from fields to a cave. If you or someone you know is new to mountain biking, this is a great place to go. It's just a nice little trail with enough technical sections to keep everyone interested. Bright yellow markers make it easy to stay on the trail. Remember, the trail is closed when wet.

HAZARDS: Expect to meet equestrians and hikers on this trail. This area is closed to all activities except deer hunting during the fall firearms season.

AREA INFORMATION: Amidst 1,479 scenic forested acres, it's hard to believe you're just a stone's throw away from Columbia. With several bubbling springs, the confluence of three streams, eight ponds, Hunter's Cave, Tumbling Cave and Spring Cave, it's no mystery why this area has been protected. Not only do you need a permit to enter Hunter's Cave, but it is also closed from April 1 through October 31 to protect grey bats.

Hawks, owls, songbirds, turkey and deer are common here. Wildflowers abound, and the forest in the fall is a must-see.

ADDITIONAL THOUGHTS: This trail is best ridden in the early spring or fall to avoid the overgrown creek banks of late spring and summer. During the spring be careful at the creek crossings. They could be in flood stage after heavy rains.

CONTACT INFO: Three Creeks Conservation Area Central Region Columbia Office, 1907 Hillcrest Drive, Columbia, MO 65201. (573) 884-6861.

DISTANCE: 12-mile loop system.

TERRAIN: Confluence of the drainage of three creeks. Hilly with several steep, technical sections.

RIDING TIME: 2½ hours.

LAND STATUS: Department of Conservation.

SERVICES & ACTIVITIES: Parking lots, no water. Primitive camping is allowed, as is fishing and hiking.

TRAILHEAD: Deer Park Road Parking Area.

RATING: Moderate to challenging.

Fred Pearson crossing Grindstone Creek. Photo by Brett Dufur.

14. GRINDSTONE NATURE AREA

NEAREST TOWN: In Columbia (Boone County).

DIRECTIONS: From the junction of I-70 and Hwy 63, go south on Hwy 63 and take the Stadium Exit. Turn west on Stadium and go to the stoplight at the bottom of the hill. This is Old Hwy 63. Turn left (south) and watch for signs on your right.

TRAIL DESCRIPTION: Numerous trails weave through this area. Everything from mowed and unmowed prairie trails to rocky, steep single-track forest sections. Two creek crossings.

HIGHLIGHTS: Several very technical hill climbs. To get there from the Old Hwy 63 parking area, cross the creek and head right a short distance through the grass then head into the woods.

CONTACT INFO: Columbia Parks & Recreation: (573) 874-7460.

DISTANCE: 6 miles of loops.

TERRAIN: Everything imaginable. From grass to loose rock. Depends on which trail you take.

RIDING TIME: 2 hours to all afternoon.

LAND STATUS: City of Columbia.

SERVICES & ACTIVITIES: Shelter and electricity. No camping.

TRAILHEAD: Off of Old Hwy 63. There are many trails across the creek and there is also a trail at the far end of the mowed area.

RATING: Easy to difficult, depending on the trail.

Jeff Scheble rides a technical section at Grindstone. Photo by Brett Dufur.

15. CAPEN PARK

BLUFFTOP & TARZAN TRAILS

NEAREST TOWN: In Columbia (Boone County).
DIRECTIONS: From the junction of I-70 and Hwy 63, take Hwy 63 south and exit at Stadium. Turn right. At the second stoplight (Rock Quarry Road/College) turn left. At the bottom of the hill, turn left onto Capen Park Road. Park at the gravel lot at the end of the road.
TRAIL DESCRIPTION: The Blufftop Trail leads to the top of the bluff. At the top, it planes out and remains a hard-packed dirt trail for more than a mile before it tapers out. To keep from backtracking, pedal this trail to its end, hit the shoulder of Stadium, go down the hill to the intersection of Stadium and Old 63, turn right, go a

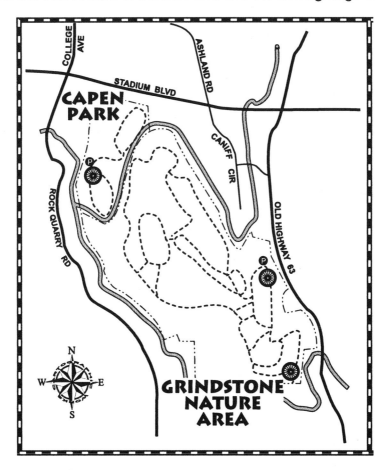

ways to Grindstone Nature Area. Take the trailhead by the parking lot, cross the creek, turn right, pedal for a bit and before you know it you'll see the Capen Park bluff across Hinkson Creek. Tip toe across the rocks in the creek and you're back!

To hit the Tarzan Trail, from the parking lot, turn right and take one of the trail accesses that will drop you down along the creek bank. This loop goes about a mile and then comes back.

HIGHLIGHTS: Good stuff. Little or no traffic. Three minutes from the center of campus and downtown Columbia.

HAZARDS: This trail gets a bit overgrown in the summer.

AREA INFORMATION: In Columbia, the bluff at Capen is the highlight of the local climbing scene. It offers 5.7 to 5.11+ climbing. Several trails run through the park, including the blufftop trail and two others that follow Hinkson Creek. If you portage across, you will be pedaling through Grindstone Nature Area.

ADDITIONAL THOUGHTS: Bring your climbing gear and your dog. If you don't climb, hike to the top of the bluff for a great view.

CONTACT INFO: City of Columbia Parks & Recreation Office: 874-7460 or Steve Saitta, Park Planner: (573) 874-7203.

DISTANCE: One mile or less in length. Six miles of trail are located across Hinkson Creek in Grindstone Nature Area.

TERRAIN: Dirt and gravel loop with several technical sections.

RIDING TIME: 1 - 2 hours.

LAND STATUS: City of Columbia.

TRAILHEAD: Several accesses from parking lot, to the right of the bluff. One MTB trail heads up the bluff onto a flat trail above.

RATING: Moderate.

16. ROCKHILL PARK
HIKING TRAIL
NOTE: RECENTLY POSTED CLOSED TO MTB'ERS...BUT STILL A GREAT HIKE.

NEAREST TOWN: In Columbia (Boone County).

DIRECTIONS: From the intersection of Stadium Boulevard and College Avenue/Rock Quarry Road, head north on College Avenue. Turn right at Rollins and head past the Veterinary School. As you pass Williams, keep an eye out for the trailhead tucked in the woods. Park in the large blacktop lot behind the Vet School. This trail may also be accessed from Rockhill Road and Wilson Avenue.

TRAIL DESCRIPTION: This five-acre park preserves a heavily wooded area. More than a mile of hilly, gravel and dirt trail offers a great secluded place to ride. Steep, semi-technical sections, exposed roots and a creek crossing make this trail scenic, enjoyable and a tad bit challenging.

HIGHLIGHTS: This place is secluded and just gorgeous.

HAZARDS: Steep hills, unstable gravel and exposed roots.

AREA INFORMATION: This trail is about three minutes from the middle of the MU campus. If you pedal west on Rollins Street straight across College Avenue, you'll be at Brady Commons (pizza and Gatorade) and the MU Rec Center. Head down Ninth Street for a great selection of restaurants and delicatessens.

ADDITIONAL THOUGHTS: Be sure and keep an eye out for bipeds and quadripeds. This is a popular spot for dog-walking for the nearby college slums, where dogs entirely outnumber students.

CONTACT INFO: Columbia Parks & Recreation: (573) 874-7460.

DISTANCE: Short but scenic. Brochure says two-thirds of a mile, but you can extend that for perhaps another mile or more by exploring the dry creek bed. Several other trails are being blazed.

TERRAIN: Steep, curvy single track. Gravel and hard-pack, bog of eternal stench and more.

RIDING TIME: A half-hour of relief to a couple of hours.

NOTE: ROCKHILL PARK RECENTLY POSTED CLOSED TO MTB'ERS... BUT STILL A GREAT HIKE.

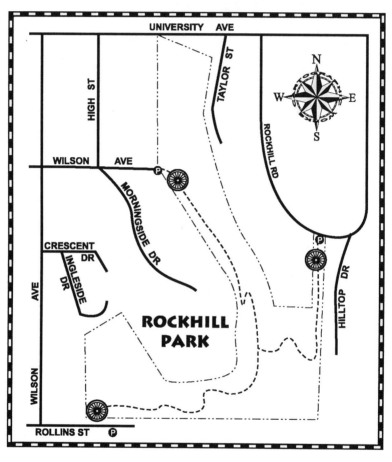

LAND STATUS: City of Columbia.
SERVICES & ACTIVITIES: Columbia has everything nearby from camping and bike repair to mocha drinking motorcycle gangs.
TRAILHEAD: On Rollins Street, across from the big blacktop parking lot behind the Vet School. Look for the overgrown trailhead with a sign in the woods directly across the road. There are also trailheads on Wilson Avenue and Rockhill Road.
RATING: Moderate.

17. COSMO RECREATION AREA
BEAR CREEK TRAIL

NEAREST TOWN: In Columbia (Boone County).

DIRECTIONS: Take I-70 to the West Boulevard Exit. Go northeast a mile to the entrance to Cosmopolitan Park, which will be on your right. Or, from I-70, take the Stadium Exit north, turn right on the first outer road and turn left into Cosmopolitan Park. Follow the signs in the park to Bear Creek Trail.

TRAIL DESCRIPTION: There is currently a short off-road trail here for mountain biking, with another, more challenging trail called Rhett's Run is in the process of being constructed. The new trail will have moderately technical sections that will add immeasurably to the range of mountain biking available within close proximity to Columbia. Under the Green Belt Acquisition, this trail is in the first phase of construction. It will eventually connect Cosmo Park with Albert Oakland Park. Plans in Columbia are also underway to connect this area with both the MK&T Fitness Trail and several other established bike routes.

CONTACT INFO: Call the Columbia Parks & Recreation at (573) 874-7460 for the latest update on the Rhett's Run Trail.

DISTANCE: 1.5 - 2 miles of trail currently. New trail will extend this by several more miles.

TERRAIN: Partly hilly.

RIDING TIME: One hour.

LAND STATUS: Columbia Parks & Recreation.

SERVICES & ACTIVITIES: Cosmo Park is also a popular site for baseball leagues, softball, basketball and has many well-managed services such as restrooms, water, picnic tables and more.

TRAILHEAD: Follow the Bear Creek Trail signs to the north end of the park.

RATING: Easy to moderate. The new Rhett's Run Trail under construction will be moderate to difficult.

18. MK&T FITNESS TRAIL

SPUR TRAIL FROM
COLUMBIA TO THE KATY TRAIL

NEAREST TOWN: Trail goes from Columbia to McBaine. In Columbia, the trail is accessible from several intersections. Accessible from Katy Trail State Park in McBaine.

DIRECTIONS: From Highway I-70 at Columbia, take the Stadium Boulevard Exit south. You will cross several major intersections including Worley, Broadway and Forum. A short distance past the Forum intersection, go downhill and at the bottom, turn right into the MK&T/Martin Luther King Park parking lot.

TRAIL DESCRIPTION: This spur trail links Columbia hikers and bikers to the Katy Trail State Park in McBaine. The flat, finely packed chat surface resembles the surface of the Katy. The scenery is beautiful, with the trail hidden beneath a shadowy archway of trees for much of its way down into the McBaine river bottoms. It starts at the Katy Station Restaurant, located at the corner of Broadway and Providence, which was once Columbia's train depot, and which now serves great food. At mile marker 0.0, just blocks from Cycle Extreme, the city is constructing a new trailhead park.

From the Katy Trail in McBaine, this trail is west of the Perche Creek railroad bridge, just a short distance west of the parking lot. Look for the "Hindman Junction" sign and the gravel trail.

HIGHLIGHTS: The MK&T Fitness Trail (short for the Missouri, Kansas & Texas Railroad line that once used this right-of-way) is a popular place for Columbia bikers and joggers. On gorgeous days, this trail is very popular.

As mentioned earlier, this area is heavily forested and the trail passes over Hinkson Creek many times as it zig zags its way to the Missouri River. Only a few blocks from the Stewart Road trailhead in Columbia is a microbrewery called Flat Branch Pub and Brewing Company. Their outdoor seating is definitely biker-friendly, and the beer sampler is a great way to pick a new favorite—perhaps you'll go home with a pint of their Katy Trail Pale Ale.

If you ride the entire distance, you will cross several bridges, and pass Twin Lakes Recreation Area's lake with sand beaches. Another definite highlight is in McBaine. Take the only road through town and head right to the 350-year-old Great Burr Oak tree.

HAZARDS: Drinking too much at Flat Branch and forgetting why you ever donned your cycling shorts in the first place.

AREA INFORMATION: Columbia is a great town. In addition to ample dining, lodging, art galleries and a great downtown, there are also many bike shops for tune-ups or trade-ups. Off of the Katy Trail or the MK&T Fitness Trail, the closest is Cycle Extreme, at 19 South 6th Street, near the Flatbranch Trailhead, or Tryathletics, north of the Forum Boulevard Trailhead at 1605 Chapel Hill Road.

CONTACT INFO: Call the Columbia Convention and Visitors Bureau at (573) 875-1231 for information on trails and for area camping options. Or Columbia Parks & Recreation at (573) 874-7460.

DISTANCE: 8.9 miles.

TERRAIN: Flat. Hard-packed chat (fine gravel) surface. Mild.

RIDING TIME: One hour.

LAND STATUS: Cooperative venture between the City of Columbia Parks & Recreation and Boone County.

SERVICES & ACTIVITIES: Everything in Columbia. Trailhead parking lot and food and water at Betty's Bar & Grill in McBaine.

TRAILHEAD: The most popular trailheads are at Stewart Avenue and Providence Road; the Martin Luther King Park on Stadium Boulevard (between Forum Boulevard and Providence Road); the Forum Boulevard Trailhead south of Chapel Hill Road and the Scott Boulevard Trailhead (head west on Broadway from Stadium into a residential area, which turns into Scott Boulevard, then go a few miles and the trailhead will be on your right).

RATING: Easy. Very flat and accessible.

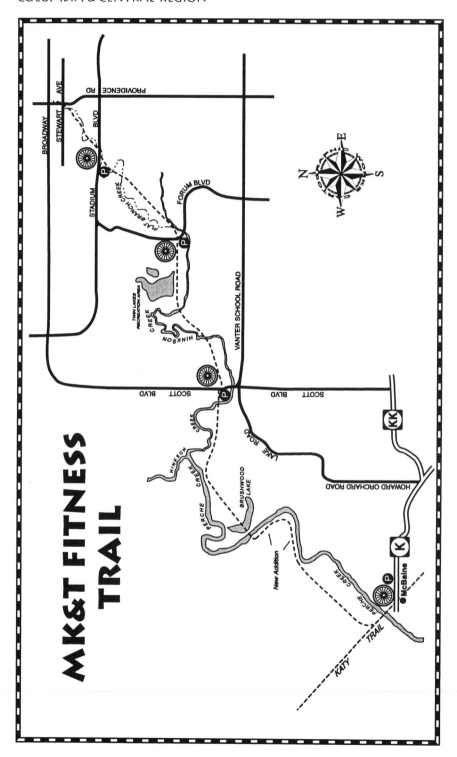

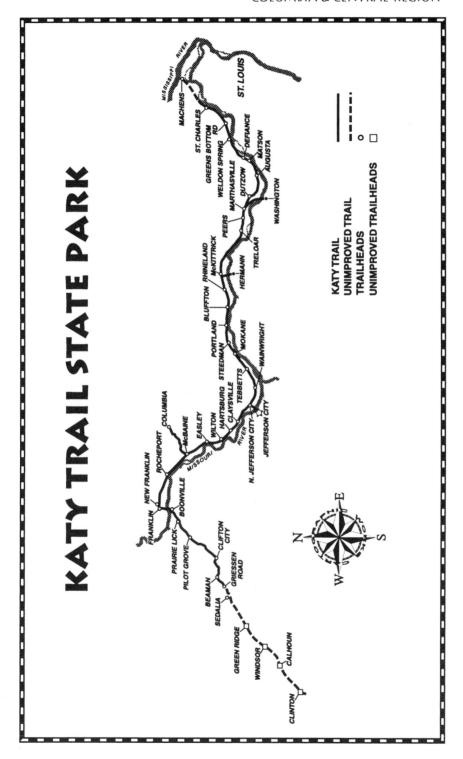

KATY TRAIL STATE PARK

KATY TRAIL
UNIMPROVED TRAIL
TRAILHEADS
UNIMPROVED TRAILHEADS

19. KATY TRAIL STATE PARK

CENTRAL REGION STOPS: BOONVILLE, NEW FRANKLIN, ROCHEPORT, MCBAINE & HARTSBURG

TRAIL DESCRIPTION: This finely packed chat surface works well for mountain bikes, hybrids and I've known many people to ride the entire 185 miles on a road bike without any problems.
HIGHLIGHTS: Bluffs, gorgeous views of the Missouri River, the Katy Tunnel in Rocheport, sunflowers, migratory birds such as the great blue heron, egrets, white pelicans and more.
HAZARDS: Beware of small washouts and soft shoulders after heavy rains. Bring some Slime™ to fix leaks caused by tiny thorns that can sometimes be picked up on the shoulders of the trail.
AREA INFORMATION: Small towns are peppered every eight to fifteen miles along this popular central stretch of the Katy Trail. Most of these small river towns have populations of 500 or less, and are great places to unwind your spring and soak in some rays. Most accomodations are bed & breakfasts. Camping is only al-

lowed in campgrounds, which there is a shortage of. The Katy Roundhouse in New Franklin has camping, and many locals can suggest a place to pitch a tent. Don't expect to see any KOA signs, though! One guy I met who had virtually pedaled the globe said the most peaceful place to camp was in cemeteries!

ADDITIONAL THOUGHTS: Eating along this stretch of trail is even more fun than riding this stretch of trail! Don't miss the cobbler at the cafe in Hartsburg, the hamburgers in McBaine or the buffalo burgers at Trailside Cafe in Rocheport.

CONTACT INFO: Department of Natural Resources: 1 (800) 334-6946 or (573) 751-2479.

DISTANCE: Expect to pedal 5-15 miles between towns.

TERRAIN: Flat. Most people prefer to ride west to east due to prevailing winds, and there is a bit of a grade from Sedalia to Boonville. From Boonville on east to St. Charles, there is a very slight downward grade of about one foot a mile.

RIDING TIME: One hour to all day.

LAND STATUS: Department of Natural Resources.

SERVICES & ACTIVITIES: Food, water and bike rentals in many towns. Call ahead if you plan on staying at area bed & breakfasts. They can fill up several months in advance. For a listing of services, refer to *The Complete Katy Trail Guidebook*, available for $14.95 by calling 1 (800) 576-7322 or call the Department of Natural Resources for their brochure. Request the free Katy Central brochure by calling 1 (888) 441-2023.

RATING: Easy.

Margo Carroll in her element. Photo by Peggy Welch.

20. MARK TWAIN NATIONAL FOREST

PINE RIDGE/CEDAR CREEK TRAIL

NEAREST TOWNS: Ashland is eight miles west, Guthrie is two miles east and Columbia is 18 miles north.

DIRECTIONS: From I-70 at Columbia go south on Hwy 63 to the Ashland/Rt. Y exit. Go left (east) on Y about 7.5 miles. Keep your eyes peeled for the Pine Ridge Recreation Area sign on your left. The trailhead is across from the parking area.

TRAIL DESCRIPTION: This trail winds its way through the hills surrounding Cedar Creek, which is a moderate to steep drainage. The total distance of the trail is approximately 22 miles. There are grey trail diamond markers throughout the trail.

The first few miles of the trail are characterized by several steep descents with hairpin turns at the bottom of some and lots of large, flat rocks and exposed roots that create many drop-ins and narrow stair-step descending. One-half mile from the trailhead, you cross a forest service pasture. Remember to shut the gate behind you, so the cows don't get out.

After that, the trail becomes more difficult. The first full mile is very challenging and fast as you twist along the edge of a deep gully that funnels water into the creek below. It alternates from very fast descents to granny gears up short, steep climbs. (Not a mountain, but steep for Missouri.) You must cross a fork of Cedar Creek before continuing about 100 feet to the first short forest road section. The trail continues less than 100 yards up the forest road. From there the trail becomes a long, sustained climb that is characterized by mostly flat rocks. This portion seemed more marred by horse traffic than the first 1.5 miles and is very rough. In the summertime heat, the other six miles were left for another day.

Posion ivy isn't too bad along the trail in the summer but there are areas where it is right next to the trail.

HIGHLIGHTS: An old farm at mile 1-1.5 stands in testament to the land's past. There is a signboard with historic information about the area near the old house. However, to avoid the tick-infested tall grasses, I left the sign for another day.

HAZARDS: Watch for old barb wired fences that can be found throughout the area.

ADDITIONAL THOUGHTS: This trail would be best ridden in the fall when the weather is drier and not as hot. Beginners or faint of heart should look elsewhere or they may be walking more of this trail than riding. Anyone attempting this trail definitely needs some suspension or a very strong upper body. The roots and rocks are a constant barrage otherwise.

Be aware of your speed on the fast descents, because some of the turns can be treacherous. Also, this trail is used by hikers. If you speed around a blind corner on a steep descent, you risk greeting any approaching hikers with more than a friendly "hello." There are frequently horseback riders on this trail, as well. At the bottom of the first long descent, after crossing the field, be very aware of your speed. The bottom ends in a somewhat blind corner and six-foot drop-off into the fork in the creek. It's a definite portage situation unless you like really, really big air.

CONTACT INFO: Cedar Creek Ranger District, 4965 County Road 304, Fulton, MO 65251.

DISTANCE: 22 miles.

TERRAIN: It's all wooded, hard-packed dirt single track that could be very slick when wet. There are a few areas that follow, for short distances, graveled forest roads. This trail is also used by equestrians, therefore, it can be very rough in spots.

RIDING TIME: 5½ hours.

LAND STATUS: Mark Twain National Forest.

SERVICES & ACTIVITIES: Camping, fishing, canoeing, hunting.

TRAILHEAD: Pine Ridge Recreation Area, Dry Fork Campground, Rutherford Bridge, Boystville, and various other parking areas throughout the district.

RATING: All skill levels will find something to challenge them here. The majority of the trail is moderately technical and the largest climb is less than 150 vertical feet, but there are areas that are more challenging.

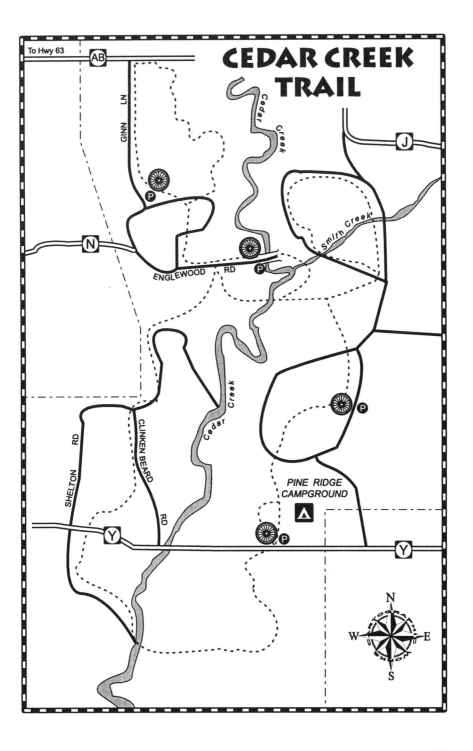

CEDAR CREEK TRAIL

To Hwy 63

AB

GINN LN

Cedar Creek

J

N

ENGLEWOOD RD

Smith Creek

P

P

P

Cedar Creek

CLINKEN BEARD

SHELTON RD

RD

RD

PINE RIDGE CAMPGROUND

Y

P

Y

N
W E
S

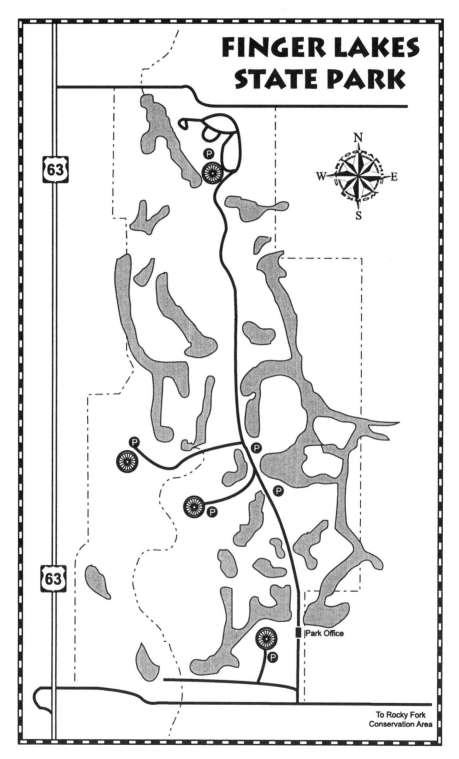

FINGER LAKES STATE PARK

If you like extremes, you will love Finger Lakes. Photo by Terry Barner.

21. FINGER LAKES STATE PARK

VARIOUS TRAILS

NEAREST TOWN: Columbia (Boone County).
DIRECTIONS: From Columbia head north on Hwy 63 for 10 miles. Look for a small sign for Finger Lakes on the east (right) side of the highway. Follow this approximately 1 mile east and turn left at the sign. If you end up at Rocky Fork Lakes Conservation Area you have gone too far.
TRAIL DESCRIPTION: The trails here are also open to motorcycles, so they are rough and loose. There are also numerous steep (read: vertical) drop-offs. More than 70 miles of off-road motorcycle trails wind through the western section of the park. The steep hills and deep ravines, remnants of strip mining, will challenge the skills of even the most experienced riders. Not all of these are MTB passable. Be wary of motorcross bikes flying around. All ATVs are required to have 6-foot high orange flags, but based on the rigs I saw without a flag, it seems Wal-Mart musta been out. Keep your eyes and ears open.

Finger Lakes is one of two state parks where all-terrain vehicles are permitted off the normal roadways. A special motocross course and staging area are on the west side of the park. Nearly a dozen motocross and motorcycle racing events are held each summer and fall in Finger Lakes State Park.

HIGHLIGHTS: No one seems to care about the condition of the trails. Riding in the mud is permitted (even encouraged). No mountain bike could do as much damage as a motocross bike, so go crazy and ride like a wild-person. This is where you can do all those nasty moves that get you in trouble elsewhere.

There is an annual race here called the White Knuckle Classic and the race course is closed to motorcycles that day. Not only is the race excellent, but it's a great day to ride the trails without having to watch for motorcycles.

HAZARDS: Natural forces can create unknown hazards. Ride with care at all times. Also, ruts left from motorcycles can turn as hard as concrete during dry summer months, making it harder to control your bike—so ride aware. Full suspension is definitely a plus here.

AREA INFORMATION: The 1,132-acre park was once a coal strip-mining area. Its regeneration shows how reclaimed strip-mine lands can be used for recreational purposes. As you pedal across the 70 miles of interwoven trails here, you will agree—this is definitely a man-made landscape. Unnaturally steep hills, straight drops, vicious turns and boundless choices are but few of the reasons this is one of central Missouri's MTB highlights.

Between June 1964 and October 1967, the Peabody Coal Co. removed more than 1.2 million tons of coal from this northern Boone County site. Left in the wake were barren piles of earth and numerous water-filled pits. Peabody replanted and reseeded much of the mined acreage and stocked several fishing lakes. The rugged terrain created by the mining, however, was not altered.

Shortly after passage of modern land reclamation laws in 1972, the U.S. Department of the Interior began searching for strip-mined sites abandoned prior to the laws on which to conduct reclamation for recreation projects. In May 1974, Peabody donated 1,028 acres of the former Mark Twain Mine to the state park system. That same month, the state received one of only a dozen federal grants to demonstrate the use of strip-mined land for recreational purposes.

ADDITIONAL THOUGHTS: There are trails, but riders can roam freely at many points too. Helmets here are highly advised. Another advantage of Finger Lakes is the relative absence of poison ivy along the trails. You may want to call ahead. If there is a motocross race, you may be hard-pressed to find an open camp site.
CONTACT INFO: Finger Lakes State Park, Columbia, MO 65202. (573) 443-5315.
DISTANCE: 70 miles of interwoven trails.
TERRAIN: Hard packed, rough, rugged and hilly.
RIDING TIME: From one hour to all day. Make sure you leave time for a refreshing swim at the free swimming lake and beach.
LAND STATUS: Department of Natural Resources.
SERVICES & ACTIVITIES: There are 35 basic camping sites, available year-round on a first-come basis. Hot showers, modern bathrooms and water are available at the campground. A nominal camping fee is collected by park personnel. There's also your normal fare of shaded picnic tables.

In addition to your bike, bring along your swimming trunks for a refreshing, after-ride swim. A large sand swimming beach, complete with change houses and latrines, is located at the far end of the large blacktop parking lot on one of the eastern finger lakes.

If you kayak, bring it along, too. There are numerous finger-shaped lakes in the park perfect for kayaking and canoeing. About a dozen small lakes have been joined together to form a 1.5-mile-long water course between the steep wooded hills in the eastern section of the park. On Thursday nights during the warmer months, Columbia's kayakers and boaters meet here to paddle, teach newcomers and enjoy this great spot.
TRAILHEAD: For the best mountain biking, park at one of the more western parking lots or small pull-offs and get started!
RATING: Moderate to difficult.

COLUMBIA & CENTRAL REGION

22. LITTLE DIXIE
CONSERVATION AREA

BOUNDARY TRAIL

NEAREST TOWN: Millersburg (Callaway County).
DIRECTIONS: From Columbia, take Broadway (Hwy WW) 10 miles east to Millersburg. Then follow the signs. Or, from Kingdom City, take I-70 west to the Route J Exit and head south to Route RA. The area is clearly marked by signs.
TRAIL DESCRIPTION: This easy trail forms a large loop around the perimeter of this 733-acre conservation area. The trail passes the 200-acre Dixie Lake, which is great for fishing, and seven good-sized ponds. There are about 200 acres of open ground and the rest is wooded. This trail is not difficult. There are a few dips and stream crossings, but this trail can be enjoyed by beginners and experienced riders looking for a scenic ride.
HAZARDS: Unlike some conservation areas, this trail is indeed open year-round, so wear hunter's orange during hunting season or wait until hunting is over.
AREA INFORMATION: There is a boat ramp and rental, nine fishing jetties, three hiking trails and picnic areas. Leave yourself enough time to swim and rent a rowboat to enjoy this large lake.
ADDITIONAL THOUGHTS: This trail is closed to equestrians. There are only occasional mountain bikers and hikers on it.
CONTACT INFO: Missouri Department of Conservation Central Region Columbia office: (573) 884-6861.
DISTANCE: 6-mile loop.
TERRAIN: Trails are dirt, gravel and hard pack.
RIDING TIME: All afternoon.
LAND STATUS: Missouri Department of Conservation.
SERVICES & ACTIVITIES: Camping is not allowed. There are restroom facilities.
TRAILHEAD: Follow directions given above to get to conservation area. There are a total of five trailheads throughout the area.
RATING: Easy to moderate.

23. RUDOLF BENNITT CONSERVATION AREA

EQUESTRIAN TRAIL

NEAREST TOWN: Higbee (Boone, Howard and Randolph Counties).
DIRECTIONS: From Columbia, take Hwy 63 north for 18 miles. Go west on Route F for 5 miles. Go north on Route T for 2.5 miles to the entrance road on the left. Follow the gravel road west for 1.75 miles, bear right for 0.25 mile, turn left on another gravel road and travel 0.5 mile to the camping area and trail access.
TRAIL DESCRIPTION: Although primarily an equestrian trail, cyclists may use the same trails always giving right-of-way to horses.
HAZARDS: This area is remote. Plan accordingly.
AREA INFORMATION: This is a 3,515-acre area named for Dr. Rudolf Bennitt, who was instrumental in getting the Conservation Department created in the 1930s. This area is at the junction of Boone, Howard and Randolph Counties. The mostly gentle, rolling terrain is 75 percent forested. Fields of native warm-season grasses and row crops are scattered among the forests. Leave plenty of time to hike the primitive Moniteau Wilderness Trail.
ADDITIONAL THOUGHTS: Bicycles are permitted only on roads and trails open to vehicular traffic and horseback riding and on service roads posted closed to motorized vehicles, except when further restricted by posting.
CONTACT INFO: Missouri Department of Conservation Central Region Columbia office: (573) 884-6861.
DISTANCE: 12 miles of gently sloping trails wander through this area—this is not a loop. Keep your bearing, since several of these trails fork, connect and abruptly stop at road crossings.
TERRAIN: Trails are primarily gentle slopes, ranging from 700 to 850 feet of elevation.
RIDING TIME: All afternoon.
LAND STATUS: Missouri Department of Conservation.
SERVICES & ACTIVITIES: Primitive camping is allowed. There are no restroom facilities.
TRAILHEAD: Follow directions given above to get to the trailhead.
RATING: Easy to moderate.

24. PRAIRIE HOME CONSERVATION AREA

EQUESTRIAN TRAIL

NEAREST TOWN: Prairie Home (Cooper and Moniteau Counties).
DIRECTIONS: This area is approximately 4 miles southwest of Prairie Home. From Prairie Home, take Hwy 87 south for 0.5 mile, go south on Route D for 2 miles, turn right on Hunt Mill Road and go to the area entrance and parking lot.
TRAIL DESCRIPTION: Although primarily an equestrian trail, cyclists may use the same trails always giving right-of-way to horses.
AREA INFORMATION: This is a 1,461-acre tract with trails that pass by several ponds and streams. Schaaf Creek runs through this area as do 13 small ponds and three lakes. About 700 acres are in timber and 520 acres are old fields, briars and warm-season grasses. The remaining 200 acres are in crops.
ADDITIONAL THOUGHTS: Bicycles are permitted only on roads and trails open to vehicular traffic and horseback riding and on service roads posted closed to motorized vehicles, except when further restricted by posting.
CONTACT INFO: Contact the Missouri Department of Conservation Central Regional Columbia Office: (573) 884-6861.
DISTANCE: 6 miles.
TERRAIN: Hard-pack dirt and some rocky sections.
RIDING TIME: One hour.
LAND STATUS: Missouri Department of Conservation.
SERVICES & ACTIVITIES: Primitive camping is allowed. No restrooms or drinkable water available.
TRAILHEAD: At area entrance.
RATING: Moderate.

25. SCRIVNER ROAD CONSERVATION AREA

EQUESTRIAN TRAIL

NEAREST TOWNS: Russellville is three miles to the north. Jefferson City is also nearby (Cole County).

DIRECTIONS: From Russellville, go south on Route AA and turn left on Scrivner Road. Go 1.25 miles, turn left on Scott Road and go one mile to parking area. From Jefferson City, take Hwy 54 west for 10 miles. Go north on Route D for 6.5 miles, west on Route C for 4 miles, then south on Route AA for 2 miles. Turn left on Scrivner Road, go 1.25 miles, turn left on Scott Road, go one mile and park.

TRAIL DESCRIPTION: From the eastern parking lot off of Clibourn Road, an extensive new horse trail in the eastern range of this 919-acre conservation area creates a large loop between the Russellville Branch of the Moreau River and South Moreau Creek. The area was a cattle farm and was extensively grazed. It is now managed for wildlife and public recreation. This trail passes through several drainages leading into South Moreau Creek, and crosses several seasonal creeks. Although primarily an equestrian trail, cyclists may use the same trails always giving right-of-way to horses.

HIGHLIGHTS: Winegar Lake is a central feature of the area, as are more than two miles of South Moreau Creek frontage.

AREA INFORMATION: Parts of this area were donated by Mrs. Alvon Winegar. This tract did not become public property until 1984.

ADDITIONAL THOUGHTS: Bicycles are permitted only on roads and trails open to vehicular traffic and horseback riding and on service roads posted closed to motorized vehicles, except when further restricted by posting.

CONTACT INFO: MDOC Columbia Office: (573) 884-6861.

DISTANCE: 5 miles.

TERRAIN: Rolling hills and mild to steep creek drainages.

RIDING TIME: 1 - 2 hours.

LAND STATUS: Missouri Department of Conservation.

SERVICES & ACTIVITIES: Ponds and streams for filtering water, but other than that, there's no drinking water, camping or restrooms.

TRAILHEAD: Scrivner Road and Clibourn Road parking areas.

RATING: Moderate.

26. SUGAR CREEK CONSERVATION AREA

EQUESTRIAN TRAIL

NEAREST TOWN: Kirksville (Adair County).

DIRECTIONS: Sugar Creek Conservation Area is 4 miles west of Kirksville. From Kirksville, take Hwy 63 south, then Hwy 11 west for 4 miles, then Route N south to the parking lots and trail access.

TRAIL DESCRIPTION: This area is primarily forested with a few open fields on ridges and along Sugar Creek. Both Sugar and Elm Creeks run through the area. Due to the grazing goats that lived here for quite some time, part of the area is still known as "goat ranch." Although primarily an equestrian trail, cyclists may use the same trails always giving right-of-way to horses.

HIGHLIGHTS: White-tailed deer and wild turkey are abundant here, as are numerous songbirds.

AREA INFORMATION: This is a 2,609-acre conservation area. If you need to bail from the trail, both Route N and Route II pass along the borders of this area.

ADDITIONAL THOUGHTS: Bicycles are permitted only on roads and trails open to vehicular traffic and horseback riding and on service roads posted closed to motorized vehicles, except when further restricted by posting.

CONTACT INFO: Department of Conservation Northeast Regional Kirksville Office: (660) 785-2420.

DISTANCE: 10.5 miles of trail.

TERRAIN: Half of this area is prairie and the other half is forested. Even the tall grass sections are passable. This is a hard-pack trail that goes over rolling hills. Nothing extreme.

RIDING TIME: 2 hours.

LAND STATUS: Missouri Department of Conservation.

SERVICES & ACTIVITIES: No restrooms or drinkable water. Primitive camping is permitted.

TRAILHEAD: The parking lots and trail access are on Route N.

RATING: Easy to moderate.

27. CHARLIE HEATH MEMORIAL CONSERVATION AREA

EQUESTRIAN TRAIL

NEAREST TOWN: Luray (Clark County).

DIRECTIONS: This area is near the Iowa border, about 15 miles northwest of Kahoka and eight miles north of Luray. To get to the trailhead from Kahoka, travel west on Hwy 136 for eight miles to Luray. Go north on Route AA for 0.25 mile, go north on Route K for 9 miles, then turn right on gravel road and go to the MDOC parking lot. The eastern side, which does not have any trails, has an access from Hwy V, 5 miles west of Hwy 81.

TRAIL DESCRIPTION: This five-mile loop is in the western portion of this area. The trail crosses the Burnt Shirt Branch of the Fox River, and goes up and down several easy to moderate drainages.

AREA INFORMATION: An initial donation of 120 acres in 1975 by sportsman Charlie Heath established this area. The Conservation Department has consequently purchased more land to bring the total area to 1,635 acres. The area is 90 percent forested. More than four miles of the Fox River meander through the area.

ADDITIONAL THOUGHTS: Trail is only open from the end of spring firearms turkey season through September 30. Bicycles are permitted only on roads and trails open to vehicular traffic and horseback riding and on service roads posted closed to motorized vehicles, except when further restricted by posting.

CONTACT INFO: MDOC Kirksville Office: (660) 785-2420.

DISTANCE: 5 miles.

TERRAIN: Gently rolling timbered hills and remnant stands of native grasses, wetlands, streams, shallow ponds and a cottonwood plantation. An active heron rookery can be found along the Fox River in the southeast region. Wildlife management techniques noticeable here include strip cropping, farming, terracing, timber harvest, controlled burning, wetland development and haying.

RIDING TIME: 1 - 2 hours.

LAND STATUS: Missouri Department of Conservation.

SERVICES & ACTIVITIES: Primitive camping. No restrooms.

RATING: Moderate.

28. DEER RIDGE
CONSERVATION AREA

EQUESTRIAN TRAIL

NEAREST TOWN: Lewistown (Lewis County).

DIRECTIONS: From Kirksville, take Hwy 6 east for 43 miles. Go north on Route H for 5.5 miles, then north on Route Y for 2 miles to County Road 355 on the right. Follow County Road 355 for 1.5 miles to the campground and trail access.

TRAIL DESCRIPTION: Although primarily an equestrian trail, cyclists may use the same trails always giving right-of-way to horses.

HIGHLIGHTS: This 4,755-acre area includes many scenic miles of moderate horse trail riding. The trails wind throughout the conservation area, in oak and hickory forest almost the entire time.

HAZARDS: This is a popular hunting spot. Wear hunter's orange during hunting season and call ahead for more information on who you may meet in the woods.

AREA INFORMATION: The Deer Ridge area was long inhabited by Native American tribes. Artifacts indicate that at least five different tribes once lived in this area.

ADDITIONAL THOUGHTS: There are 25 ponds in case you need to filter water or want to fish. Bicycles are permitted only on roads and trails open to vehicular traffic and horseback riding and on service roads posted closed to motorized vehicles, except when further restricted by posting.

CONTACT INFO: Missouri Department of Conservation Northeast Region Hannibal Office: (573) 248-2530.

DISTANCE: A nine-mile trail that crisscrosses back over itself, creating three loops.

TERRAIN: Classic moderately challenging creek drainages. Trail follows ridge lines, as well as crossing into several valleys.

RIDING TIME: 3 hours.

LAND STATUS: Missouri Department of Conservation.

SERVICES & ACTIVITIES: Primitive camping is permitted at four designated campgrounds. Restroom facilities are available.

TRAILHEAD: Follow the signs.

RATING: Moderate.

NOTES:

_____

_____

_____

_____

_____

_____

_____

_____

_____

_____

_____

_____

_____

_____

_____

_____

_____

_____

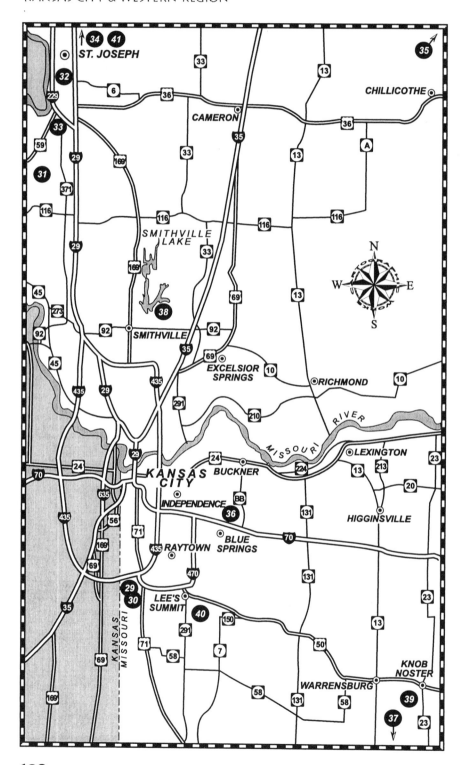

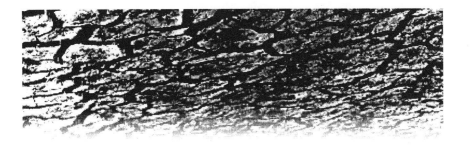

KANSAS CITY & WESTERN REGION TRAILS

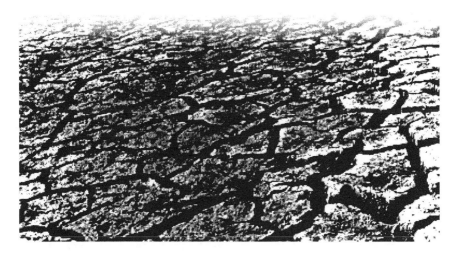

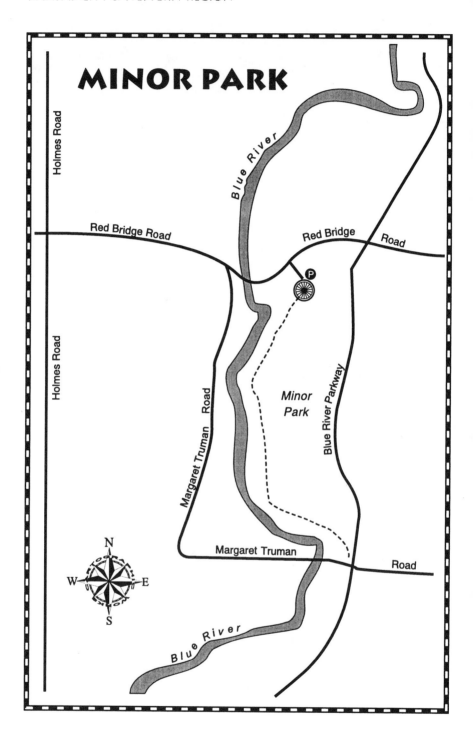

MINOR PARK

29. MINOR PARK

VARIOUS TRAILS

NEAREST TOWN: In southern metro Kansas City area.
DIRECTIONS: At the south end of the I-435 loop, take I-435 (east/west) to the Holmes Road exit. Go south on Holmes to Red Bridge Road (Burger King on left, Minor Park Golf course across the bridge and to the left). Go left (east) on Red Bridge, across the—you guessed it—red bridge. Park entrance is first right past the bridge.
TRAIL DESCRIPTION: Minor Park has several miles of trails to choose from. You'll need to ride it a couple of times to pick out your favorite route. Don't stop at river or street crossings, there's probably more trails on the other side. It helps to hook up with

someone who has ridden there before and can show you around. The route I take is about 10.5 miles there and back and runs the gamut from wide easy cruising to tight winding through the woods with several creek and river crossings (2 creek, 4 river), a couple of moderately technical spots and a nice downhill or two.

HIGHLIGHTS: There's a couple of fun sections that twist and wind through the woods. To get to the first one, when you come up on the river for the first time, instead of crossing, go left. The second is on the other side of Blue Ridge Boulevard. Also on the other side of Blue Ridge is a section with a fun, somewhat tricky descent mixed with a couple of short rocky climbs. Trying to cross the Blue River without putting a foot down is fun—the moss can be slick.

HAZARDS: Watch for fallen trees, poison ivy hugging the trail and mud bogs with steep banks on the other side.

AREA INFORMATION: This multi-use park has basketball courts and a shelter. There's no real parking lot at the trailhead, just a cul-de-sac, but its OK to park here. Remember this is an urban trail, so expect to see urban people in the woods.

ADDITIONAL THOUGHTS: When you come to Blue Ridge Boulevard, in the woods to the right is a trail that will take you under this street. Much better than crossing it. Also, if there's a train when you come to the railroad tracks, there is a trail that goes up and over. Minor Park trails are shared with horseback riders; remember the rules of the trail. It takes about a week for these trails to dry out after a good rain.

CONTACT INFO: Kansas City Department of Parks & Recreation: (660) 871-5600. If you mention this MTB trail, they won't know what you're talking about. If you call and ask for directions to the *golf course,* which is nearby, then they can help you out.

DISTANCE: 8 - 12 miles of interwoven trails.

TERRAIN: Wooded, wide, hard-packed trail, mud holes, steep descents and creek and river crossings.

RIDING TIME: One hour to all afternoon.

LAND STATUS: City park.

SERVICES & ACTIVITIES: Nearby golf course, Burger King and anything else you might need is probably within 20 minutes.

TRAILHEAD: Enter Minor Park, drive to the end and park at the cul-de-sac-looking parking lot near basketball courts. Head over the grassy knoll to the trail that heads up a steep rise. Trails weave all over from there.

RATING: Easy to moderate.

YOLT!! (You Only Live Twice!)
Joe Martin drops in for a 20-foot "cold one." Photo by Brett Dufur.

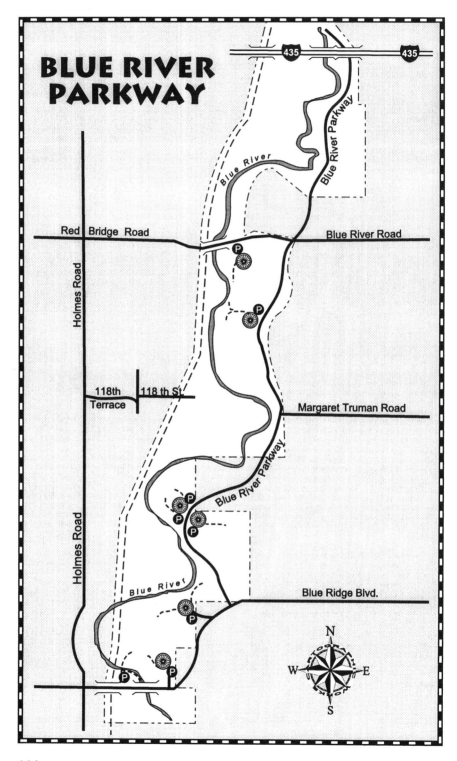

BLUE RIVER PARKWAY

30. BLUE RIVER PARKWAY

VARIOUS TRAILS

NEAREST TOWN: Martin City, one mile southwest. This is a suburb of Kansas City (Jackson County).

DIRECTIONS: To get to the access points, take I-435 west to Holmes Road, turn south on Holmes Road, go 3.5 miles to Blue Ridge Boulevard, then east 0.25 mile. The area is on the left. There are three entry points for this ride.

TRAIL DESCRIPTION: Many bluffs and trees along this trail. Flat to rolling hills with an occasional ridge here and there, none more than 10 feet high. There is a short section of trail that follows along the railroad tracks. Stay on the east side of the tracks and the trail picks back up about 50 yards away.

HIGHLIGHTS: It's hard to believe you're in the city with all of the woods and bluffs along this trail. This is an easy getaway from city life and a good place to train for longer rides.

HAZARDS: Be sure and watch for joggers.

AREA INFORMATION: 5-acre protected area.

CONTACT INFO: Call the Jackson County Parks Department at (816) 795-8200.

DISTANCE: Two miles one-way.

TERRAIN: Flat to rolling hills.

RIDING TIME: One hour one-way.

LAND STATUS: County park.

SERVICES & ACTIVITIES: No camping. Fishing, hiking, restrooms, parking, pavilion and boat ramp.

TRAILHEAD: Trailhead at parking lot.

RATING: Easy.

31. BLUFFWOODS CONSERVATION AREA

BLUFFWOODS HORSE/MTB TRAIL

NEAREST TOWN: St. Joseph (Buchanan County).

DIRECTIONS: From St. Joseph take Hwy 59 south for 9 miles. Look for the Bluffwoods Conservation Area sign and turn left. Take this gravel road for a mile to an intersection and go right. Now heading south, go left when you reach a fork in the road. The trailhead is a few yards east of the circle gravel parking lot. The trailhead has a horse trail sign there.

TRAIL DESCRIPTION: This is a short but demanding course, mostly through woods but with spots of pasture. The whole thing is single track. Rutted sections made by horses and several steep, rocky sections make it a trail for experienced riders only. As mentioned before, this trail is also a horse trail. Therefore it is rugged and marred by hoof prints. There are some VERY difficult, rocky climbs. In fact you'll probably have to dismount at various points. There are also numerous technical descents. The length is about three miles. While there isn't much tight, twisting single track, this trail provides an excellent workout.

HIGHLIGHTS: About halfway through, the trail leads into a clearing on top of a ridge. There you will enjoy a good view of the surrounding countryside, including the Missouri River and its floodplain. Look for wild turkey, deer and other species of wildlife.

AREA INFORMATION: The Department of Conservation purchased this 2,400-acre area in the mid-1970s to protect one of the last large, heavily wooded areas in northwest Missouri.

ADDITIONAL THOUGHTS: Make sure you're in shape if you're planning on riding this trail. Also, suspension of some kind is recommended. I ride a hardtail, but I was wishing I was on a Y-33 or a Team LTS. The rocky descents are very unforgiving so don't be surprised if you go endo. Also there are some small sapling stumps littering the trail here and there so make sure you keep an eye out for them. If you are the first one to ride the trail on any given day you can expect numerous spider webs in your face. This may be a good place to let your buddy take the lead!

CONTACT INFO: MDOC Northwest Region Office, 701 NE College Drive, St. Joseph, MO 64507. (816) 271-3100.

DISTANCE: 3-mile loop.
TERRAIN: Steep. The fine soil (loess) on this trail gives and erodes very easily.
RIDING TIME: One hour.
LAND STATUS: Department of Conservation.
SERVICES & ACTIVITIES: St. Joseph is several miles north. The Forest Nature Hiking Trail nearby is paved. Restrooms and a shelter house are available to campers and picnic groups. Primitive camping, fishing, hiking, horse trail and mushroom hunting.
TRAILHEAD: At parking lot.
RATING: Challenging.

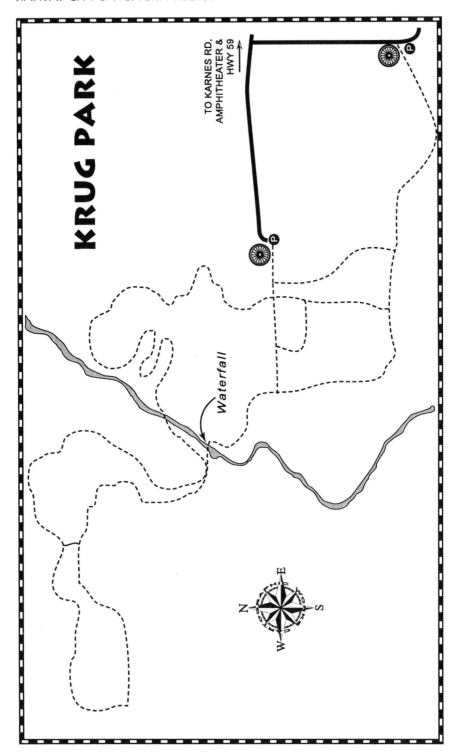

32. KRUG PARK

KRUG PARK TRAIL

NEAREST TOWN: St. Joseph (Buchanan County).
DIRECTIONS: From St. Joseph head west on Hwy 59 (St. Joseph Avenue). You will find Krug Park along Karnes Road.
TRAIL DESCRIPTION: This trail is for all skill levels. It's mainly hard-packed, hilly single track with a few creek crossings. A few trails loop through this area, totaling close to three miles, allowing you to circuit train to your heart's content. The waterfall at the end of the long downhill is the most challenging section of the ride.
HIGHLIGHTS: Waterfall, fountains and lagoon.
AREA INFORMATION: This scenic park has a large, idyllic lagoon with fountains, which serves as a focal point for the road, tunnel, trails and other highlights throughout the park. There is an amphitheater, wild animal preserve, gardens and more.
CONTACT INFO: St. Joseph Parks Department: (816) 271-5500.
DISTANCE: 3-mile system.
TERRAIN: Hilly, hard-packed single track.
RIDING TIME: One hour.
LAND STATUS: City park.
SERVICES & ACTIVITIES: Water and camping.
TRAILHEAD: The trailhead/parking lot is on the west side of the park, at the back of the park just north of the buffalo pens.
RATING: Easy to difficult, depending on trail.

33. SOUTHWEST PARKWAY TRAILS

VARIOUS TRAILS

NEAREST TOWN: Southwest St. Joseph (Buchanan County).
DIRECTIONS: In the north end of town. From Hyde Park, take the Southwest Parkway and park just south of the I-229 underpass. The trail is contained within about a mile south of here on the west side of the Parkway.
TRAIL DESCRIPTION: This small wild area is a popular spot for MTB'ing, ATVs and equestrians. About five miles of single track wind around with a few really steep sections. The trails are mainly hard packed and will be muddy after a rain. Elevation changes are from 850 to 1,000 feet. Most climbs are ridable by cyclists in good condition. No stream crossings to freeze your feet in the winter.
HIGHLIGHTS: You're never more than 500 yards from civilization. Never seems to be crowded.
HAZARDS: Other than a few washouts, no hazards.
AREA INFORMATION: Historic St. Joe has some of the most

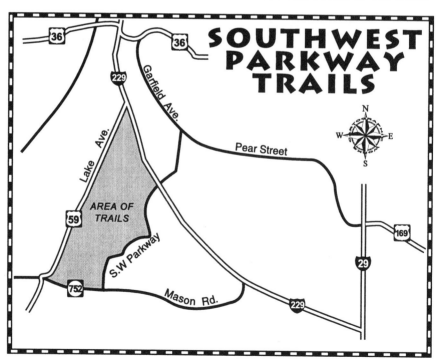

amazing architecture I've seen. Stop at the Visitors Center down-town and leave time to explore this often-overlooked destination.
ADDITIONAL THOUGHTS: This is a good ride any season.
CONTACT INFO: St. Joseph Department of Parks: (816) 271-5500.
DISTANCE: 5-mile system.
TERRAIN: Hilly but do-able.
LAND STATUS: City park.
SERVICES & ACTIVITIES: No water near trail. St. Joe is nearby.
TRAILHEAD: Park on the side of the road just south of the I-229 underpass.
RATING: Easy to moderate.

KANSAS CITY & WESTERN REGION

34. RIVERBREAKS CONSERVATION AREA

EQUESTRIAN TRAIL

NEAREST TOWNS: St. Joseph & Forbes (Holt County).

DIRECTIONS: From St. Joseph, take I-29 north. Turn onto Hwy 59 north (Exit 67) and go 3.5 miles. Go south on Route O for 3 miles, then turn right on the gravel road and go to the parking lot. To reach the west tract, continue south on Route O to Forbes, go west 4.5 miles on Route T, turn down the Beastie Boys, then park.

TRAIL DESCRIPTION: Although primarily an equestrian trail, cyclists may use the same trails always giving right-of-way to horses.

AREA INFORMATION: This 2,307-acres area is nestled among the river bluffs overlooking the Missouri River floodplain. Numerous creeks and streams wind through the area, and there are many ponds along the trail.

ADDITIONAL THOUGHTS: Even though brochures say this area does not allow MTB's on horse trails, they do. There is a new horse trail system that winds throughout the conservation area. Bicycles are permitted only on roads and trails open to vehicular traffic and horseback riding and on service roads posted closed to motorized vehicles, except when further restricted by posting.

CONTACT INFO: Missouri Department of Conservation Northwest Regional St. Joseph Office: (816) 271-3100.

DISTANCE: 8 miles.

TERRAIN: Hardpacked dirt and several rocky sections.

RIDING TIME: 1 - 2 hours.

LAND STATUS: Missouri Department of Conservation.

SERVICES & ACTIVITIES: Sorry. No restrooms, but primitive camping is permitted.

RATING: Moderate.

122 — SHOW ME MOUNTAIN BIKING

35. POOSEY CONSERVATION AREA

EQUESTRIAN TRAIL

NEAREST TOWN: Chillicothe (Livingston County).

DIRECTIONS: From Chillicothe, take Hwy 65 north to Hwy 190 west and go 2 miles to Route A. Go north for 9 miles to County Road 511, then north on County Road 511 to the parking lot and trail access.

TRAIL DESCRIPTION: There are 18 miles of winding trail here, that do not all connect up. Instead, they meander throughout this conservation area, passing through different drainages and near several pioneer cemeteries. Indian Creek Community Lake is a great spot to cool off after a hard ride, so bring your swimming trunks. Although primarily an equestrian trail, cyclists may use the same trails always giving right-of-way to horses.

AREA INFORMATION: This 5,591-acre area contains unique fern-draped stone walls, heavily timbered hills of oak and hickory, rolling grass expanses and a variety of wildlife. This portion of the Grand River Valley was one of the last parts of Missouri yielded by Missouri's Native American tribes. In 1833, the last remnants of the Shawnee tribe left the area, under continued pressures from settlers arriving from Kentucky, Tennessee and Virginia.

The area's rugged landscape reminded some of the settlers of the Poosey region in Kentucky, hence the name.

ADDITIONAL THOUGHTS: Bicycles are permitted only on roads and trails open to vehicular traffic and horseback riding and on service roads posted closed to motorized vehicles, except when further restricted by posting.

CONTACT INFO: Missouri Department of Conservation Northwest Region Chillicothe Office: (660) 646-6122.

DISTANCE: 18 miles of winding trail.

TERRAIN: Steep, forested hills. Hardpack, grassy and rocky trail.

RIDING TIME: 3 - 4 hours.

LAND STATUS: Missouri Department of Conservation.

SERVICES & ACTIVITIES: Primitive camping allowed in designated areas only. No restrooms or potable water available. Bring your water filter or bring in plenty of water.

RATING: Difficult.

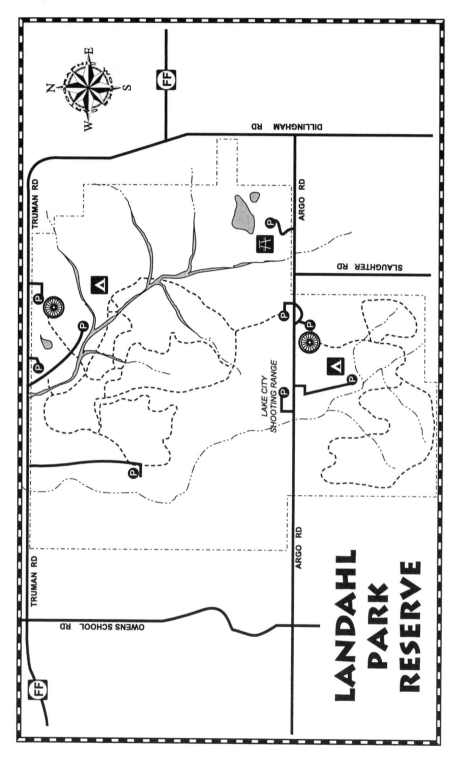

Photo by Peggy Welch.

36. LANDAHL PARK RESERVE

MTB TRAILS

NEAREST TOWN: Blue Springs (Jackson County).
DIRECTIONS: Exit I-70 at Highway 7. Take 7 north to Argo Road. There is a sign there identifying the Missouri Department of Conservation's Lake City Range. Turn right (east) here. Follow this rather cruddy road until you go past the gun range on your left. You will go up a hill, look for the gravel parking lot and shelter to your right. Park here. The MTB trails can be found by crossing the road and following the double track into the woods. The MTB trail is marked as "Dave's Maze." If you see the Oakland United Methodist Church on your right, you've gone too far.
TRAIL DESCRIPTION: This trail is a nine-mile loop comprised almost entirely of nice, tight single track. The course here will throw everything at you; extremely technical rocky stretches, sketchy climbs up loose and rocky slopes, long smooth descents where the only limit on your speed is your guts, and correspondingly long lung-busting climbs.

The front part of the trail is pretty gentle but the back part is not for the faint of heart. There are several stretches of very difficult, tight and windy rocky passages with some decent drop-offs and tough areas where just navigating the path without dabbing is about all you can hope for . . . as for taking these parts at speed . . . forget it.

HIGHLIGHTS: I'm not that great of a rider but I love the tough spots. The trails are heavily wooded and quite pretty. I also enjoy tough climbs and these trails have several that are very tough, but if you know what you're doing (which I don't) you can clean them.

HAZARDS: A few of these trails loop behind the Lake City shooting range. There are huge berms to catch the bullets and there seem to be no immediate safety risks, but—thought you might want to know.

AREA INFORMATION: The Truman Road Trailhead begins across a cable bridge. The shelter and pond here make a nice place to take a break. The beginning of this ride is pretty flat, and heads into shaded, wooded gorgeous hills.

ADDITIONAL THOUGHTS: Even though it is just a nine-mile course, plan on a good two-hour ride for a decent rider's first trip through. Once you are more familiar with the course you will be more comfortable hammering through the easier sections and it won't take as long.

This trail stays just horribly muddy for a ridiculously long time. I rode here a full week after any significant rain and it was a miserable bog. However in the fall and spring it is very beautiful.

CONTACT INFO: Jackson County Parks and Recreation, 22807 Woods Chapel Road, Blue Springs, MO 64015. (816) 795-8200 or (816) 650-3257. Physical address of park office is 28015 E. Truman Road, Independence, MO.

DISTANCE: 5-mile loop.

TERRAIN: Mostly flat with a few great hills. Gentle to granny gear.

RIDING TIME: 2 hours.

LAND STATUS: Jackson County Parks and Recreation.

SERVICES & ACTIVITIES: Picnic tables, softball, soccer and horseback riding. Fishing, shelter, primitive restrooms, no water.

TRAILHEAD: Truman Trailhead (parking lot off Truman Road) and the Argo Trailhead at the Argo Road Shelter.

RATING: Moderate to difficult.

37. KATY TRAIL STATE PARK

SEDALIA

Sedalia is currently the western-most trailhead for the Katy Trail. A 33-mile section is nearing completion that will connect the Griessen Road Trailhead to Sedalia, pass the State Fairgrounds and continue on to Clinton. This soon-to-be-completed section may also have a test section for horseback riding.

From Sedalia to Boonville, the Katy passes through prairie and gradual, rolling hills, until it meets up with the Missouri River valley in Boonville. This is the most solitary stretch of trail and there is a slight grade from Sedalia heading east. (I didn't notice it, but a friend *really* noticed it when towing two kids in a Burley cart.)

CONTACT INFO: Call the Department of Natural Resources for more information at 1 (800) 334-6946.

DISTANCE: 185 miles (one-way).

TRAILHEAD: Griessen Road. From the only "real" intersection in Sedalia (Hwy 50/65), take Hwy 50 east 11 blocks to Engineer. Turn north, then cross the railroad tracks, pass the cemetery, turn right and go about two miles to the trailhead on the right.

RATING: Flat and easy.

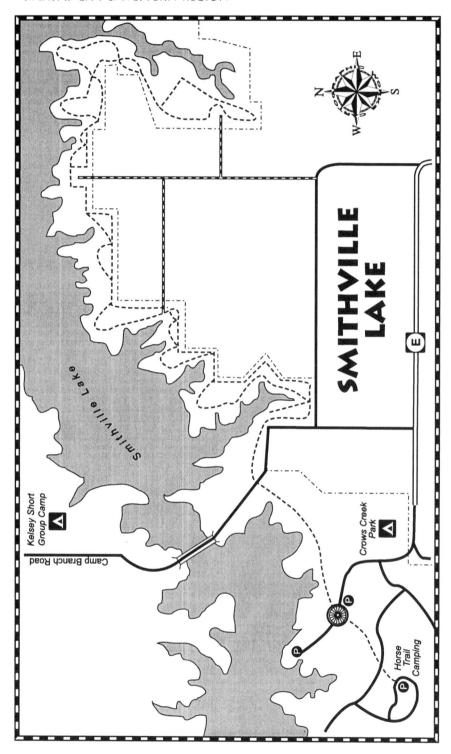

38. SMITHVILLE LAKE

EQUESTRIAN TRAIL

NEAREST TOWN: Smithville (Clay County).

DIRECTIONS: Take I-435 north to I-169 north and follow the signs to Smithville Lake. Then follow signs to Crows Creek Park.

TRAIL DESCRIPTION: The Shoreline Trail (orange markers) is 10 miles long and the Boundary Trail (white markers) is six miles. The two trails converge at several points, allowing you to loop back to your car in most instances without having to backtrack.

These trails are almost more theoretical than actual—a map exists to this trail, there are trail markers—but as one ranger puts it, this trail is *"au naturel."* Meaning they don't mow it, work on it, zip, nada. Let's just put it this way, my first time out there I was at the trailhead for 20 minutes checking out deer trails before I finally found the trail markers—green metal fence posts with white-painted tips—passing through the nearby prairie. Other areas of the trail are more clearly marked with landscape timbers with a horseshoe on them (pointing up to catch the good luck).

While some trails are double track or single track, this trail is *no* track. As its name implies, this is more of a horse trail, so equestrians might not even pay attention to two-foot-high grass, which would sure catch the chagrin of MTB'ers.

HIGHLIGHTS: You're right next to the lake in areas of relative solitude, which lets you soak in lesser-appreciated areas of this immensely popular lake and take a short swim whenever the whim hits you like a discounted pumpkin after Halloween.

HAZARDS: Just the normal ticks and skeeters.

AREA INFORMATION: This man-made lake was created beginning in 1979 by damming the Platte River. Today, with a surface area of more than 7,000 acres, Smithville Lake is a popular spot for fishermen, boaters and outdoor lovers of all varieties.

ADDITIONAL THOUGHTS: For a combined great training ride and a day sunning on a sand beach, this place can't be beat.

CONTACT INFO: Jerry L. Litton Visitor Center, 16311 DD Highway North, Smithville, MO 64089. (816) 532-0174 or (816) 532-0803.

DISTANCE: Shoreline Trail, which has orange markers, is 10 miles long. The white-markered Boundary Trail is 6 miles long.

TERRAIN: Grassland prairies, gravel, edges of woods and gully and water crossings. Sections of this trail are not heavily trodden, leading to that "overgrown" feel.

RIDING TIME: 3 hours.

LAND STATUS: Clay County Parks and Recreation/U.S. Army Corps of Engineers.

SERVICES & ACTIVITIES: Smithville Lake and Recreation Area is huge. All of the necessities are nearby, from camping and hospitals to pizza joints. Camping is available at Crows Creek Campground, (816) 532-0803, nearby and several others. Services include water, restrooms and showers. Follow the signs around the lake to the various campgrounds. Pricing is comparable to other state parks. Fire rings and grills are available but I'd advise bringing some wood with you.

TRAILHEAD: Trailheads at Accesses 22, 23 and 24 are clearly marked on all maps of the lake. Also, you may reach the trails by setting up camp at the Crows Creek Park. Last time I was there, however, the people at the greeting booth of Crows Creek Park said MTB wasn't allowed on this trail. After a few phone calls, however, the Corps of Engineers responded with a resounding yes it is. This confusion will hopefully not detract from your attempts to ride this 100% legal MTB trail.

RATING: Moderate. Difficulty depends on the season ridden.

Keep your eyes peeled for these silent, skinny, sometimes hard-to-see trail markers. Several stretches are marked with posts that have horseshoes on them (pointing up to catch the good luck).

39. KNOB NOSTER STATE PARK

MCADOO EQUESTRIAN TRAIL

NEAREST TOWN: Knob Noster (Johnson County). Next to Whiteman Air Force Base.

DIRECTIONS: From Warrensburg take Hwy 50 east for 7 miles until you see Hwy 132, then go south. At Route DD, go west and you'll arrive at the parking lot for the McAdoo Equestrian Trail.

TRAIL DESCRIPTION: The mountain biking trail is a seven-miler developed for MTB and equestrian use. For hikers, there are trails varying in length from one-half to two miles that wind through the park's forested areas, along the lake shores and into native grass-land areas. The Boy Scouts also maintain a compass trail through the park, so if you want to hone those rusty compass skills, contact the park office for necessary maps.

HIGHLIGHTS: Passing through large stretches of trail without sharing a single gorgeous view with anyone.

HAZARDS: Tall grass can make trails challenging to virtually im-possible depending on when they were mowed last.

AREA INFORMATION: The diverse landscape, clear streams and abundant wildlife of the Knob Noster area attracted Indians as early as 7,000 years ago. One of the legends of these Indians helped to give Knob Noster its name. The area was named for the two hills northeast of town. The Indians called these hills "knobs," and leg-end relates that the mounds were constructed as monuments to slain warriors following an Indian war. Settlers later added the word "noster," which comes from a Latin word meaning "our." So, "our knob" became Knob Noster.

Much of the park's natural beauty and landscape diversity is influenced by Clearfork Creek, which meanders through the area. The 3,567-acre park features a nature center with exhibits, several small lakes, a small stream, a wooded campground, an equestrian trail and camp and two group camps—Camp Shawnee and Camp Bobwhite. A mixture of prairie grasses and widely spaced trees form a park-like savanna landscape here. The Pin Oak Slough Natu-ral Area is a four-acre forested oxbow slough that forms a small wetland along Clearfork Creek.

The park is located in the Osage Plains, which are dominated by prairie landscape. Because of the creek's drainage, the area around the park is dissected and hilly, with a wide corridor of trees following the creek through the prairie landscape.

Although remnants of the once-extensive prairie and savanna landscapes remain, the majority of the park is covered by thick second-growth forests. White oak, northern red oak, shagbark hickory, redbud and red mulberry dominate the upland areas of the park, while bur oak, pin oak, walnut, sycamore and hackberry are found in the richer bottomland areas. Wildlife is abundant in the park and includes white-tailed deer, fox, raccoon, opossum, wild turkey, barred owl, pileated woodpecker and frequent sightings of the great blue heron.

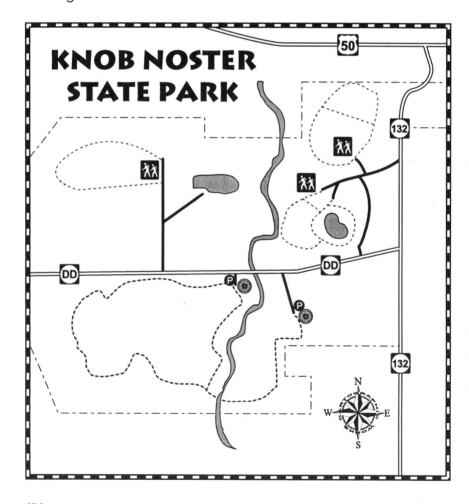

ADDITIONAL THOUGHTS: Finding out information by phone will be impossible unless you refer to "the equestrian trail." Although this trail is MTB legal, you'll get more information if you tell them your mode of choice is a horse.
CONTACT INFO: Knob Noster State Park. Knob Noster, MO 65336. (816) 563-2463
DISTANCE: 7 miles
TERRAIN: Mostly flat.
RIDING TIME: One hour.
LAND STATUS: Department of Natural Resources.
SERVICES & ACTIVITIES: Restrooms, camping, fishing and picnicking. This state park has 33 basic and 40 improved campsites available year-round in a wooded area of the park. Facilities include modern restrooms, hot showers and laundry facilities. A daily camping fee is charged, on a first-come basis. Campers receive a discount between November and March. The campgrounds and picnic areas are wheelchair accessible. In the campground, water is turned off from November 1 through the end of March.

Whiteman Air Force Base, located next to the park, manages the Royal Oaks Golf Course, which is also available to park users.

Two organized group camps in the park may be used by non-profits organizations and youth groups who apply in advance with the park superintendent. Camp Shawnee has accommodations for 150 campers and Camp Bobwhite has accommodations for approximately 167 campers. Facilities include cabins, a dining lodge and kitchen, a swimming pool and other outdoor facilities.

There are also 75 picnic sites scattered throughout the park and near the lakes. Three open picnic shelters and playground equipment are also provided.

Bring your pole if you want to fish for channel catfish, bass and bluegill. Small boats without motors are allowed on Lake Buteo and Clearfork Lake.
TRAILHEAD: Parking lot on Hwy DD.
RATING: Easy.

40. JAMES A. REED MEMORIAL WILDLIFE AREA

EQUESTRIAN TRAIL

NEAREST TOWN: Lee's Summit (Jackson County).

DIRECTIONS: From Lee's Summit, take Hwy 50 east to Ranson Road (RA). Turn south and go 1.5 miles to the entrance on the left.

TRAIL DESCRIPTION: Although primarily an equestrian trail, cyclists may use the same trails always giving right-of-way to horses. Interestingly enough, horseback riders require a daily permit, but mountain bikers can ride here without a permit. Stick to the roads and horse trails. The trail is a 15-foot-wide swath through this 2,603-acre area, that is mostly level for easy to moderate riding. A local hiking trail leads to an interesting limestone outcrop.

AREA INFORMATION: This area was established in 1952 when Mrs. Reed donated 731 acres in memory of her husband, Senator James A. Reed. Additional tracts brought the area to 2,603 acres. More than 250 acres of water have been impounded to form 12 lakes, the biggest of which is 42 acres. If you like fishing bring your pole, since these lakes are stocked with channel cat, bluegill, striped bass hybrids, sunfish and bullheads. Giant Canada geese nest and winter here, and the area also supports a large deer population.

ADDITIONAL THOUGHTS: Be sure and check out the area set aside as a butterfly and hummingbird garden. Bicycles are permitted only on roads and trails open to vehicular traffic and horseback riding and on service roads posted closed to motorized vehicles, except when further restricted by posting.

CONTACT INFO: MDOC Kansas City Office: 13101 Ranson Road, Lee's Summit, MO 64082. (816) 524-1656.

DISTANCE: 12-mile trail.

TERRAIN: Primarily flat. Kept pretty clear of brush. Remember the builders had horses in mind when they built this trail, so it might not be ideally suited for bike riding if it hasn't been mowed or cleared lately. But why not check it out anyway?

RIDING TIME: 2 hours.

LAND STATUS: Missouri Department of Conservation.

SERVICES & ACTIVITIES: Camping is prohibited. There are restrooms. No drinking water is available.

RATING: Easy to moderate.

41. HONEY CREEK CONSERVATION AREA

EQUESTRIAN TRAIL

NEAREST TOWN: Savannah (Andrew County).
DIRECTIONS: 15 minutes north of St. Joseph on I-29. Take the Filmore Exit and go left on Route RA, which takes you right to it. This area is located on the west side of I-29 before it crosses the Nodaway River. Or, from Savannah, go about four miles east on Hwy E, then go six miles north off of Hwy D. Look for the bright yellow boundary sign and the big sign along the road.
TRAIL DESCRIPTION: This is a new horse trail. Although primarily an equestrian trail, cyclists may use the same trails always giving right-of-way to horses.
AREA INFORMATION: Rolling hills, with a few technical spots, forested oak and hickory
ADDITIONAL THOUGHTS: Bicycles are permitted only on roads and trails open to vehicular traffic and horseback riding and on service roads posted closed to motorized vehicles, except when further restricted by posting.
CONTACT INFO: Department of Conservation Northwest Region St. Joseph Office: (816) 271-3100 or try (816) 675-2205.
DISTANCE: 10 miles of loops and counterloops.
TERRAIN: Mowed grass and hard pack trail. There are also several creek crossings.
RIDING TIME: 2 - 4 hours.
LAND STATUS: Missouri Department of Conservation.
SERVICES & ACTIVITIES: No water or restrooms. Primitive camping is allowed.
TRAILHEAD: Several trailheads can be found throughout the area.
RATING: Easy to moderate.

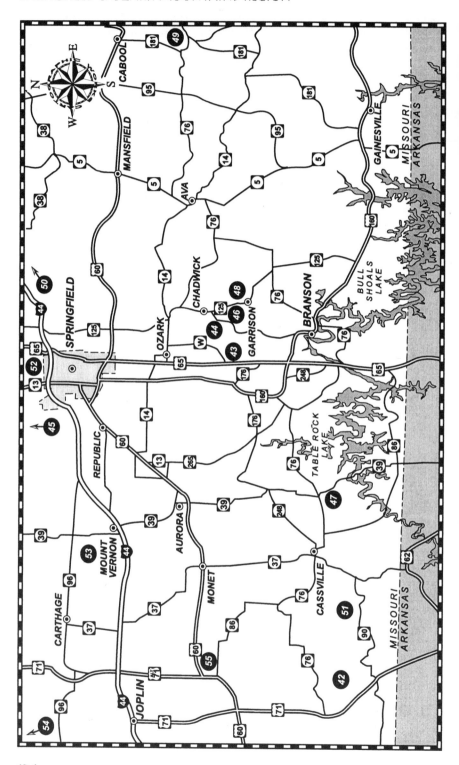

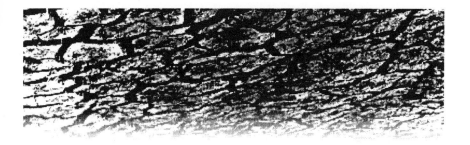

SPRINGFIELD & OZARK MOUNTAINS REGION TRAILS

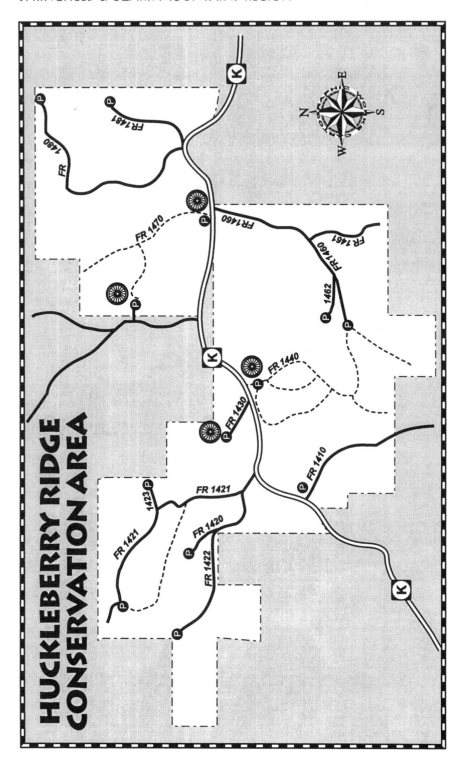

HUCKLEBERRY RIDGE CONSERVATION AREA

FR 1481

FR 1480

FR 1470

FR 1460

FR 1461

FR 1460

1462

FR 1440

FR 1430

FR 1410

1423

FR 1421

FR 1421

FR 1420

FR 1422

42. HUCKLEBERRY RIDGE CONSERVATION AREA

VARIOUS TRAILS

NEAREST TOWNS: Neosho and Joplin are 25 to 40 miles away. (McDonald County).

DIRECTIONS: Head south out of Pineville on Hwy 71. Take Route K east four miles. This takes you all the way to the Huckleberry Ridge Conservation Area.

TRAIL DESCRIPTION: Single and double track, climbs and descents—no markers but the trail is very self-explanatory. This area is very similar to Flag Spring. Typical Ozark forest with highly variable trails combining riding on public, ridge and logging roads and game trails.

HIGHLIGHTS: This is classic Ozark trail riding. There are a few sections for moderate riders but the majority of this steep trail is for experts.

HAZARDS: Be careful on the steep and loose sections of the single track, foot trails and horse trails.

AREA INFORMATION: Covering 2,100 acres, this conservation area includes a cave, a spring and five ponds. This Ozark mountain area is densely wooded and very hilly.

ADDITIONAL THOUGHTS: Mountain bike races are held here each year. Call the number below for more information.

CONTACT INFO: Huckleberry Ridge Conservation Area, Cassville Forestry Office, P.O. Box 607, Cassville, MO 65625. (417) 847-5949.

DISTANCE: 18-mile system.

TERRAIN: Mostly hilly. The trails here are composed of loose native rock.

RIDING TIME: 3 - 5 hours.

LAND STATUS: Department of Conservation.

SERVICES & ACTIVITIES: No water's to be had in the forest but you can primitive camp at will.

TRAILHEAD: Park at either parking area or at the primitive camping site.

RATING: Moderate to extremely technical.

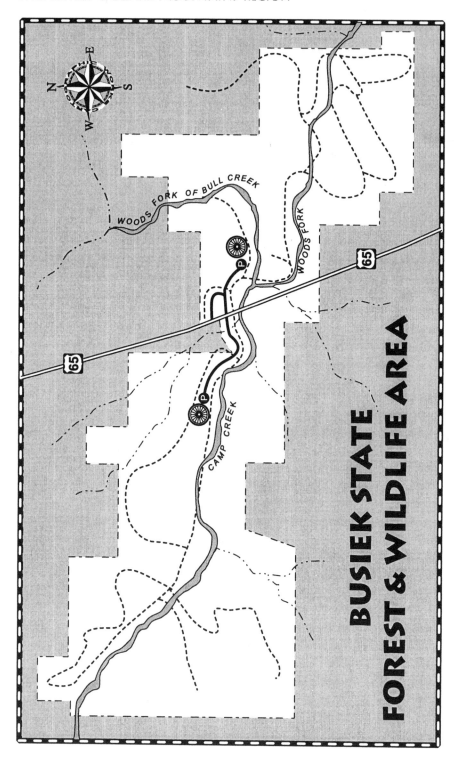

43. BUSIEK STATE FOREST & WILDLIFE AREA

NEAREST TOWN: Springfield 18 miles north (Christian County).

DIRECTIONS: From Springfield, go south on Hwy 65 about 18 miles and watch for Busiek's easily missed sign. There is one sign on the right, but the entrance to the conservation area is on the left side at the bottom of a very steep hill, so don't look at the sign too long. A second area access is 1.5 miles further south on Hwy 65. Turn east on Route A and go less than 0.25 mile, then go north on a one-lane gravel road for 0.25 mile to the parking area.

TRAIL DESCRIPTION: 14 miles of flat and easy trail to highly technical sections and stream crossings. These trails have everything! From long, flat, winding trail on the western side, which forms two good loops, to rocky climbs and dangerous drops on the east.

HIGHLIGHTS: The ridges here are all unique, offering spectatular view of the Ozarks or quiet old pioneer cemeteries. In the summer the rivers are great for swimming.

HAZARDS: Several parts of the trail are extremely steep and technical. Also, don't attempt any portages if the creeks are up.

AREA INFORMATION: This heavily forested 2,505-acre conservation area is the drainage of three miles of Camp Creek and Woods Fork of Bull Creek. There are 13 ponds for fishing and close to 300 acres of glades. Hawks, owls, songbirds, turkeys, deer and rabbits are common here, as are wildflowers and mushrooms.

ADDITIONAL THOUGHTS: No water. This is a great place to ride in all seasons. While it gets kind of muddy after rain, once you get to the higher elevations it is just wet rocks (is that a good thing?). Also, there is a drop-off in the northeast section of the trail that I almost broke my hand trying to ride. Be careful!

CONTACT INFO: Conservation Department's Springfield Office, 2630 N. Mayfair, Springfield, MO 65803. (417) 895-6880.

DISTANCE: 14-mile system.

TERRAIN: Flat to extreme drops. Loose rocky terrain and hard pack.

RIDING TIME: 3 - 4 hours.

LAND STATUS: Department of Conservation.

SERVICES & ACTIVITIES: Primitive camping, fishing and hiking. Nearby Bass Pro Shop is always worth a visit. Where else can you buy a camouflaged ski mask and order a Big Mac!? *Viva Missouri!*

RATING: Easy to challenging.

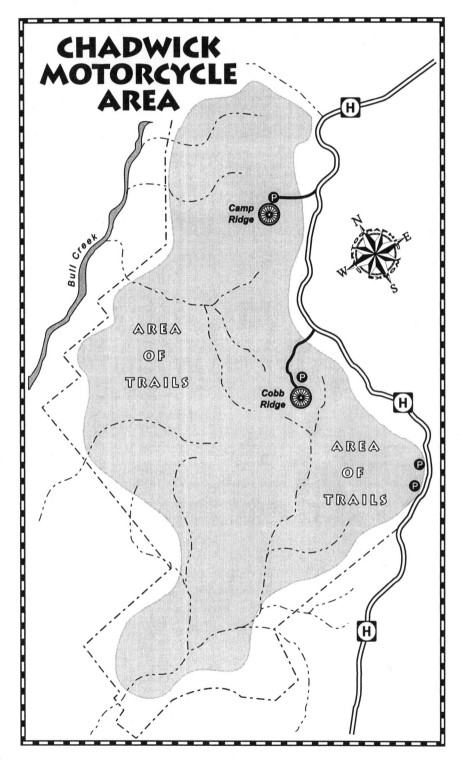

CHADWICK MOTORCYCLE AREA

Bull Creek

Camp Ridge

Cobb Ridge

AREA OF TRAILS

AREA OF TRAILS

44. MARK TWAIN NATIONAL FOREST

CHADWICK MOTORCYCLE AREA

NEAREST TOWN: Chadwick (Christian County).
DIRECTIONS: From Hwy 60 take Hwy 125 south 20 miles to County Road H, just past Chadwick. A bit down H you'll reach the trailhead at Camp Ridge & Cobb Ridge. Or, take Hwy 65 south to Hwy 14 east. Go about 15 miles to Hwy 125 south to Chadwick, just south of the town is a junction for Highway H. There will be a sign for Chadwick ATV area. Park in the parking/camping areas.
TRAIL DESCRIPTION: Well-marked and numbered trails. According to one rider who lived and raced in Colorado, this was the most technical riding area he had ever seen. Most of the moderate track is usually attached to some extremely technical downhill section. There's also loose gravel in the low areas. One rider I talked to had ridden more than 100 miles of trails over three days without duplicating trail. He recommended against full suspension and clipless pedals. Another rider, however, recommends some suspension and that clipless pedals work fine. There is a lot of stuff here that the motorcycles can't even get through.
HIGHLIGHTS: It's so big that you don't run into people much, and the motorcycles make enough noise that you can get out of their way. Rattlesnake Cave has a bridge that is worth a stop. The motorcycle riders are usually very nice to MTB's, they will usually give you water (you'll need a refill if you get far away from camp).
HAZARDS: Low spots often muddy. Washouts. Don't exceed your experience level. Know your limits.
AREA INFORMATION: You need a permit to ride trails here. Revenues pay for maintenance and improvement of the area. Permits may be purchased at the Forest Service office, or Kay's Store.
ADDITIONAL THOUGHTS: Make sure you have a map every time you go out there. The trails are confusing and it is easy to get lost. My third chainring was never used. You can camp there for free (primitive camping) at Camp Ridge, or for a fee at Cobb Ridge (developed campground). Keep your eyes peeled for copperheads.

Greg Bolinger is a frequent rider at Chadwick. Photo by Neal Dufur.

Mountain Bike Magazine rates Dairy Queen Hill as nine inches of plush travel and very technical. With skill, you can do it with two.
CONTACT INFO: MTNF Ava Ranger District (417) 683-4428.
DISTANCE: 125-mile system of interconnecting trails.
TERRAIN: Hilly. This area is hard on equipment.
RIDING TIME: All day to several days.
LAND STATUS: Mark Twain National Forest.
SERVICES & ACTIVITIES: Camping, restrooms, shelter. Chadwick has a small store; Springfield is an hour away.
TRAILHEAD: At parking lot. Watch for signs.
RATING: Some areas are easy, but most of the trail is moderate to challenging. Best ridden on weekdays to avoid the weekenders.

45. SAC RIVER TRAIL

NEAREST TOWN: Springfield (Greene County).
DIRECTIONS: From I-44, go 3 miles on Hwy 13 north. Follow signs.
TRAIL DESCRIPTION: One of the newest additions to Missouri mountain biking, this trail consists of an outer loop with spoke-like, more difficult trails heading into the center. For those familiar with the area, this trail is located immediately across the river from the now-closed Ritter Springs City Park. Ritter Springs' trail is closed due to overuse by hikers, bikers and equestrians.

The Sac River Trail is located on a 300-acre city tract. This project is an excellent example of one community answering the needs of its outdoor enthusiasts. With the assistance of Terry Whaley and the crew at Ozark Greenways, this trail became a reality with cooperation between Springfield Parks and Recreation, Public Works and the Fire Department. About 95 percent of the effort to create this trail has been done by area riders plus a cadre of international volunteers here on CIEE exchange programs.

These trails offer a variety of challenges. Damien Wardien told me that he took part in a 12-hour three-man team race here and never got sick of it. Others have told me this is a great place to learn how to mountain bike, especially if you stick to the inside trails.

HIGHLIGHTS: Rough downhills, best with suspension.
HAZARDS: There's a bomb disposal area nearby, where old dynamite and the occasional pipe-bomb are destroyed.
ADDITIONAL THOUGHTS: Open during daylight hours. Efforts are being made to allow limited night riding. Also, right at the gravel lot, there's a few loops and jumps for young kids.
CONTACT INFO: Terry Whaley at Ozark Greenways, P.O. Box 50733, Springfield, MO 65805. (417) 864-2014. Or, call the Springfield Greene County Park Board at (417) 864-1052.
DISTANCE: About 6.5 miles of single track, which will be extended.
TERRAIN: Mixture of terrain. Be prepared for above average technical difficulty. Fun but rough. Some trails are more technical due to their narrowness. There are also a couple of smooth trails to pick up speed. Several creek crossings. Easy to navigate.
RIDING TIME: One quick outer loop lap to all day.
LAND STATUS: City of Springfield.
SERVICES & ACTIVITIES: Plans include to build a shelter and restrooms and to make water available onsite.
RATING: Moderate to difficult, depending on which trail you take.

46. MARK TWAIN NATIONAL FOREST

DEVREAUX RIDGE TRAIL

NEAREST TOWN: South of Chadwick (Christian County).
DIRECTIONS: Located six miles south of Chadwick, on County Road H. At Devreaux Ridge Road and Garrison Ridge intersection.
TRAIL DESCRIPTION: This trail is primarily a double-track gravel road. These are seldom used forest roads, more than a MTB trail, per se. They have many easy to moderate sections, as well as several more challenging unmaintained stretches and crossings of Garrison Branch. It is worth checking out if Chadwick is more difficult than you anticipated. The trails here are generally beginner-friendly, with enough challenges to sedate even skilled riders.
HIGHLIGHTS: Gorgeous dogwoods and redbuds in spring. Garrison Branch has some great swimming holes.
HAZARDS: Don't attempt high-water crossings.
ADDITIONAL THOUGHTS: No drinking water available on trail. You may encounter vehicles out here.
CONTACT INFO: MTNF Ava District: (417) 683-4428.
DISTANCE: 15-mile system.
TERRAIN: Flat to hilly. Hardpacked to gravel forest service roads.
RIDING TIME: Two hours to all afternoon.
LAND STATUS: Mark Twain National Forest.
SERVICES & ACTIVITIES: Chadwick has a small store. See Chadwick Trail information. Camp at Camp Ridge or Cobb Ridge at the Chadwick Motorcycle Use Area, which is 2.25 miles north of Garrison Ridge Road on County Road H. Or, continue on to the Hercules Glades Wilderness and camp there. Take Hwy 125 south for 30 miles, then follow the signs.
TRAILHEAD: At Devreaux Ridge Road and Garrison Ridge intersection. Or, from the eastern edge of Chadwick Motorcycle Use Area, you can start at Camp Ridge and Cobb Ridge Campgrounds. From these points, take County Road H for several miles until you get to Garrison Ridge Road, heading east. Follow it 1.5 miles to Devreaux Ridge Road, which heads southeast, and get started.
RATING: Easy to challenging.

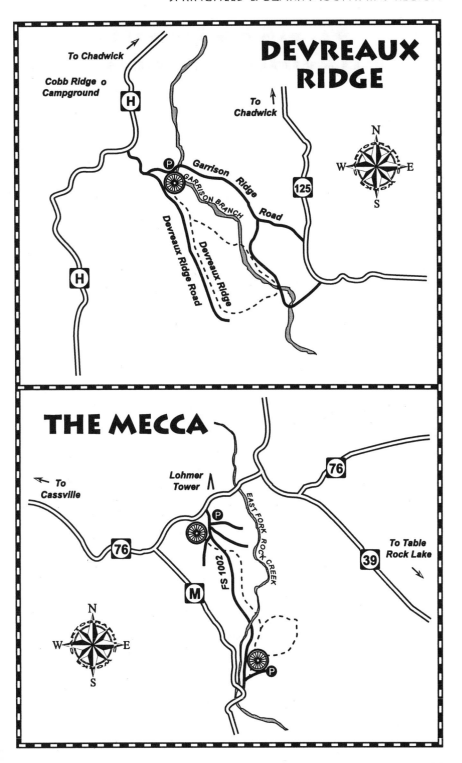

DEVREAUX RIDGE

To Chadwick

Cobb Ridge o
Campground

H

To ↑
Chadwick

N
W E
S

P

Garrison Ridge Road

GARRISON BRANCH

Devreaux Ridge Road

Devreaux Ridge

125

H

THE MECCA

To
Cassville

Lohmer
Tower ↑

76

EAST FORK ROCK CREEK

P

FS 1002

76

M

To Table
Rock Lake

39

N
W E
S

P

47. MARK TWAIN NATIONAL FOREST

THE MECCA

NEAREST TOWN: Cassville is 10 miles to the west (Barry County).
DIRECTIONS: To get to the northern trailhead, 10 miles east of Cassville, take Hwy 76 to Lohmer Lookout Tower. Park at the tower and ride 0.5 miles west to FR 1002. Turn south on FR 1002 and you're there. To enter this trail from the south, go 8 miles east of Cassville to County Road M. Go south 4 miles to the bridge and park in the field 0.25 miles north of the bridge.
TRAIL DESCRIPTION: The main Mecca route is FR 1002, which crosses about 500' of elevation. Start at the north end of the trail so that most of your ride will be downhill. This is a good ride for MTB'ers looking for trails to challenge a variety of skill levels. Beginners can stick to the main forest road double track. You will also see several bulldozer lines, or offshoots, which are fire lines. These are not considered open for riding. This trail skirts the drainage for the east fork of Rock Creek and crosses it twice.
HIGHLIGHTS: Side trails offer great wildflower viewing.
HAZARDS: This trail isn't marked, so if your navigation skills aren't the best, be sure and take a GPS or stick to the main Forest Service road double track. Also, don't cross Rock Creek if levels are high.
AREA INFORMATION: Table Rock Lake is close by.
ADDITIONAL THOUGHTS: No drinking water is available. Fun trail for group rides.
CONTACT INFO: Mark Twain National Forest, Hwy 248 West, Cassville, MO 65625. (417) 847-2144.
DISTANCE: 8 miles of double track with an abundance of side trails.
TERRAIN: Hilly.
RIDING TIME: Two hours to all afternoon.
LAND STATUS: Mark Twain National Forest.
SERVICES & ACTIVITIES: Stores in Cassville, at Table Rock Lake and in Springfield. Camping available at Roaring River State Park 6 miles south of Cassville and at other areas around Table Rock Lake.
TRAILHEAD: Park in open field, a quarter mile north of the bridge.
RATING: Easy to moderate.

SWAN CREEK TRAILS

1. Beer Can Alley
2. Math Branch Trail
3. Cedar Glade
4. Dead Horse Hill
5. Cross Creek
6. Salt Lick
7. Bald Knob
8. Greyhound Special
9. Moonshine Hollow
10. Deer Cave
11. Buckeye Hill
12. Sly Top
13. Rocky Top
14. Tin Top
15. Little Waterfall Trail
16. Chicken Thief
17. Spring House Trail
18. Dogwood Hill
19. Paw Paw Patch

48. MARK TWAIN NATIONAL FOREST

SWAN CREEK TRAILS

NEAREST TOWN: Chadwick (Christian County).

DIRECTIONS: Drive south from Chadwick on Hwy 125 for 6 miles. You'll see a sign for Bar K Wrangler Camp on the left. Turn left and follow the dirt road 0.5 mile to the trailhead.

TRAIL DESCRIPTION: Many of the trails offer easy riding but there are many areas of steep, unstable technical riding that are best portaged by inexperienced and even experienced riders.

This is a fast and rolling trail. Much of it is single track but some old logging roads are also used. Most climbs are moderate to long in length and some are unridable. There are several creek crossings so late spring, summer and fall are the best times of year to ride. There are many connected trails in the Swan Creek area. The wooded area is very secluded.

HIGHLIGHTS: Swan Creek is gorgeous. Be sure and visit Horseshoe Falls, too.

HAZARDS: Swan Creek can rise quickly during storms.

AREA INFORMATION: This area was first developed by equestrians Larry and Marian Jackson in 1978. Today the trails are fairly well marked and a graded road leads to the Bar K Wrangler Camp constructed in 1992.

ADDITIONAL THOUGHTS: Don't forget your fishing pole and license! Not recommended for winter months, due to the Swan Creek crossing right at the beginning of the ride.

CONTACT INFO: Mark Twain National Forest Ava Ranger District: (417) 683-4428.

DISTANCE: 20 + mile system.

TERRAIN: Hilly single track with some very rocky sections. The inside trails are more difficult, since they have large boulders that you have to maneuver around.

RIDING TIME: 6 hours.

LAND STATUS: Mark Twain National Forest.

SERVICES & ACTIVITIES: Swimming, fishing, horseback riding. The nearest water and services are six miles north in Chadwick.

TRAILHEAD: The trail starts on the far side of Swan Creek.

RATING: Easy to difficult.

North Fork area of the Ridge Runner Trail.

49. MARK TWAIN NATIONAL FOREST

RIDGE RUNNER TRAIL

NEAREST TOWN: West Plains (Howell County).

DIRECTIONS: From Cabool, take Hwy 181 south 16 miles. Turn onto Route AP and go southeast. The trailhead is off AP near the Noblett Recreation Area.

TRAIL DESCRIPTION: Steep and technical sections, some long climbs. The 8.8-mile Noblett loop consists of several difficult long steep climbs (many of which have switchbacks that are too steep even to ride down). Also, the trail is a little difficult to follow in some spots. But aside from these hitches, the trail has some of the best views of any biking trail I've been on in Missouri. The Noblett loop is mostly single track with a good mix of fireroads. I haven't ridden the 14-mile North Fork loop but I'd expect that the terrain is similar to that of the Noblett loop sans great views of Noblett Lake.

HIGHLIGHTS: Spring wildflowers & swimming in Noblett Lake.

HAZARDS: Parts are rocky, steep and technical.

ADDITIONAL THOUGHTS: The poison ivy and mosquitoes can be unbearable in the summer, so bring bug repellent and water to wash off with after you ride.

CONTACT INFO: MTNF Willow Springs Office: (417) 469-3155. Or, call the Ava office at (417) 683-4428.

DISTANCE: 42 miles total.

TERRAIN: Mostly hilly.

RIDING TIME: All day.

LAND STATUS: Mark Twain Forest.

SERVICES & ACTIVITIES: Water, camping and horseback riding are found at Noblett Lake and North Fork Recreation Areas; food and lodging in Willow Springs and West Plains.

TRAILHEAD: Noblett Lake Trailhead is located off Hwy AP. The North Fork Trailhead is on Hwy CC next to the North Fork River.

RATING: Moderate to challenging.

50. MARK TWAIN NATIONAL FOREST

COLE CREEK EQUESTRIAN TRAIL

NEAREST TOWN: Lebanon (Laclede County).
DIRECTIONS: From Lebanon, go east on Hwy 32 for 7 miles to Route N. You'll come to the junction of Routes AC and K. At that point go east 1.5 miles on gravel road and turn left (north) 0.25 mile to the small field on the right side (east side). Trailhead parking is in this field. There should be a trailhead sign, but there are no signs to direct you to that point.
TRAIL DESCRIPTION: This moderately challenging trail passes through the Cole Creek drainage and is 14 miles long. Rocky trail conditions. Typical Ozark hill country covered in oak and hickory vegetation and there are three ponds near the trail.
HIGHLIGHTS: This trail is used primarily by equestrians, but it offers many challenges for the curious mountain biker.
HAZARDS: Be sure and bring plenty of food, water and a complete repair kit. This trail is in the middle of nowhere.
AREA INFORMATION: This is typical Ozark topography. The trail passes through oak and hickory forests, pine plantations and is a ridge-to-valley trail.
ADDITIONAL THOUGHTS: Scenic vistas and wildflowers in controlled burn sites make this a great ride.
CONTACT INFO: Houston/Rolla Mark Twain National Forest: (417) 967-4994. In Rolla, call (573) 364-4621.
DISTANCE: 14 miles.
TERRAIN: Hardpack and loose gravel sections.
RIDING TIME: All afternoon.
LAND STATUS: Mark Twain National Forest.
SERVICES & ACTIVITIES: Hiking, biking and horse use. No developed facilities along trail. Bring your own drinking water. Paddy Creek Recreation Area is a good place to camp.
TRAILHEAD: At field off gravel road. See directions above.
RATING: Moderate.

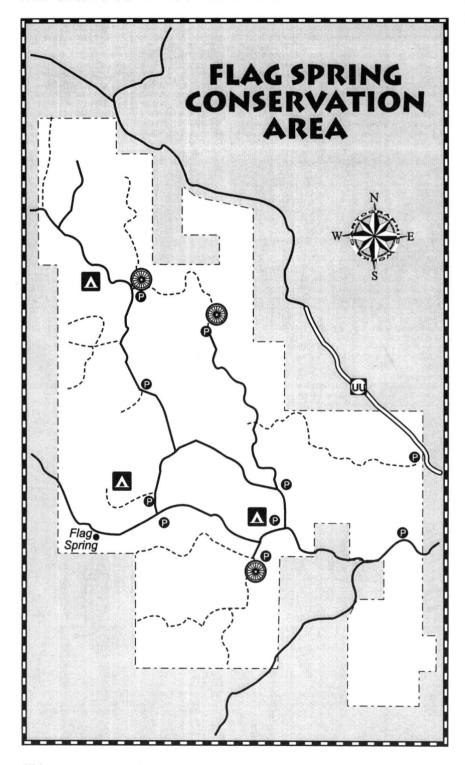

FLAG SPRING
CONSERVATION
AREA

Flag
Spring

51. FLAG SPRING CONSERVATION AREA

EQUESTRIAN TRAIL

NEAREST TOWN: Washburn (Barry and McDonald Counties).

DIRECTIONS: Flag Spring Conservation Area is northwest of Washburn about 1.75 miles on Hwy UU, then left 3 miles on the first public gravel road.

TRAIL DESCRIPTION: This series of equestrian trails is more ideally suited for horseback riders than mountain bikers in many spots, due to the wild and woolly condition of many sections of trail. This is primarily a ridge road and trail ride, which is remote and sees little usage. Trail conditions cover the gamut from good to bad. This area is similar to Huckleberry Ridge Conservation Area, in that you pass through typical Ozark forest, with highly variable trails ranging from public roads to ridge and logging roads, with some game trails. Be prepared for bushwacking in most sections. There are no real markers to guide you and when you're out there, you're *out* there.

HIGHLIGHTS: Ozark forests, interesting rock formations.

HAZARDS: No water. Bring your own and a filtration system.

AREA INFORMATION: On this 3,955-acre conservation tract, primitive camping is allowed.

ADDITIONAL THOUGHTS: There's also a shooting range on the conservation area.

CONTACT INFO: Cassville Forestry Office, P.O. Box 602, Cassville, MO 65625. (417) 817-5949.

DISTANCE: 8-mile loop but not all of it is clearly marked.

TERRAIN: Wild and woolly. Expect some bushwacking.

RIDING TIME: Short rides to all day.

LAND STATUS: Department of Conservation.

SERVICES & ACTIVITIES: Camping and hiking.

TRAILHEAD: Trailhead at parking lots.

RATING: Easy to challenging depending on the stretch.

52. LEAD MINE CONSERVATION AREA

EQUESTRIAN TRAIL

NEAREST TOWN: Camdenton (Dallas County).

DIRECTIONS: From Camdenton, take Hwy 54 west for 18 miles. Go south on Hwy 73 for 6 miles. Go east on Route E for 4 miles, go south on Route T to the area entrance sign at Route YY. Turn left, then turn left again on the first gravel road. Travel north then east for 4 miles to the horse trail parking lot. Or, from Plad, take Hwy 64 north, then Route T north and go 0.5 mile east on Hwy YY. Turn left at first gravel road, then go north for one mile to main parking area.

TRAIL DESCRIPTION: This four-mile horse trail is nestled within 7,180 acres. There is a mile of frontage on the Niangua River here, three miles of Jake's Creek, two ponds and seven springs. Mountain bikers are allowed on horse trails and more horsetrail miles are planned. Although primarily an equestrian trail, cyclists may use the same trails always giving right-of-way to horses.

HIGHLIGHTS: Gorgeous bluffs and the Niangua River, which passes through the northeast corner of this area.

HAZARDS: Be careful of steep drop-offs at bluffs.

ADDITIONAL THOUGHTS: No area brochure is available. Bicycles are permitted only on roads and trails open to vehicular traffic and horseback riding and on service roads posted closed to motorized vehicles, except when further restricted by posting.

CONTACT INFO: Missouri Department of Conservation West Central Region Lebanon Office: (417) 532-7612.

DISTANCE: 4 miles.

TERRAIN: Typical Ozark country, with rolling hills, some pretty steep creek drainages, rocky soil, mostly oak and hickory forest.

RIDING TIME: 1 - 2 hours.

LAND STATUS: Missouri Department of Conservation.

SERVICES & ACTIVITIES: Primitive camping is permitted. Restrooms available.

RATING: Moderate to difficult.

53. ROBERT E. TALBOT CONSERVATION AREA

EQUESTRIAN TRAIL

NEAREST TOWN: Mt. Vernon (Lawrence County).

DIRECTIONS: From Mt. Vernon, take I-44 west for 5.5 miles. Go north on Hwy 97 for 5 miles. Turn right on the gravel road and go to the parking lot and trail access. To reach another trail, continue north on Hwy 97 for 2.75 miles to the parking lot on the right.

TRAIL DESCRIPTION: There are two loop trails here. The 5.8-mile northern loop is the larger of the two and is accessible directly off Hwy 97, near its junction with Hwy 96. The 4.8-mile southern loop is accessible from the trailhead access off Route V heading west out of Mt. Vernon. Although primarily an equestrian trail, cyclists may use the same trails always giving right-of-way to horses.

AREA INFORMATION: In 1980, the Conservation Department purchased 246 acres to protect the riparian habitat along Spring River. An additional 4,114 acres were purchased, making for a total contiguous area of 4,360 acres. The area honors the late conservation commissioner Robert E. Talbot from Joplin. This area is predominantly open rolling hills with more timbered acreage along the river. Spring River flows unchannelized through the area's southern portion. There are also two lakes and 26 ponds.

ADDITIONAL THOUGHTS: Bald eagles are sometimes seen over Spring River, and a group of sycamores contain a great blue heron rookery with more than 100 active nests. The conservation area's brochure says Spring River supports an estimated 150 pounds of fish—smallmouth bass, channel catfish, sunfish and suckers—per acre. Bicycles are permitted only on roads and trails open to vehicular traffic and horseback riding and on service roads posted closed to motorized vehicles, except when further restricted by posting.

CONTACT INFO: MDOC Springfield Office: (417) 895-6880.

DISTANCE: 10.6 miles of horse trail.

TERRAIN: Dirt and mud along Spring River to rocky, upland soils.

RIDING TIME: 2 - 3 hours.

LAND STATUS: Missouri Department of Conservation.

SERVICES & ACTIVITIES: Camping allowed in designated areas. The one-mile nature trail meanders along the Spring River bluffs.

RATING: Easy to moderate.

54. BUSHWHACKER LAKE CONSERVATION AREA

EQUESTRIAN TRAIL

NEAREST TOWNS: Nevada & Bronaugh (Vernon & Barton Counties).
DIRECTIONS: From Nevada, take Hwy 54 west 4 miles. Turn south on Hwy 43 and go 13 miles to the area entrance on the left. Follow the gravel road east for 3.25 miles to the horse trail parking lot.
TRAIL DESCRIPTION: Today, more than 1,200 acres of prairies are being restored through controlled burning. About 120 acres of native hay meadows remain, harboring the same plant communities that buffalo once grazed.Although primarily an equestrian trail, cyclists may use the same trails always giving right-of-way to horses.
HIGHLIGHTS: Bushwhacker Lake.
HAZARDS: This trail is only open from May 15 – September 30. Wear hunter's orange.
AREA INFORMATION: During the Civil War Kansas Jayhawkers ambushed local residents believed to be Confederate sympathizers. In retaliation, those men, known as bushwhackers, banded together and started their own guerilla war against the Union. The guerrilla warfare soon spilled over into Missouri, and some fierce fighting took place along nearby Little Dry Wood Creek. So Bushwhacker is an appropriate name for this 4,417-acre conservation area, since Little Dry Wood Creek flows through the eastern portion.
ADDITIONAL THOUGHTS: Bicycles are permitted only on roads and trails open to vehicular traffic and horseback riding and on service roads posted closed to motorized vehicles, except when further restricted by posting.
CONTACT INFO: Missouri Department of Conservation Southwest Region Springfield Office: (417) 895-6880.
DISTANCE: 6 miles.
TERRAIN: Gently sloping hills.
RIDING TIME: 2 hours.
LAND STATUS: Missouri Department of Conservation.
SERVICES & ACTIVITIES: Primitive camping is allowed. Only primitive restroom facilities are available.
TRAILHEAD: Follow signs to the equestrian trails.
RATING: Moderate.

55. FORT CROWDER CONSERVATION AREA

EQUESTRIAN TRAIL

NEAREST TOWN: Neosho (Newton County).

DIRECTIONS: From Neosho, take Route HH east for 3.5 miles to the area parking lot and trailhead.

TRAIL DESCRIPTION: This 2,363-acre area is primarily forested with different species of oaks. Trails meander throughout the area, passing Gibson Spring and a dozen ponds. Elevations here range from 1,100 to 1,300 feet above sea level. The area is bordered on the north by Route HH, on the south by Route D and on the east and west by county roads. If you need to bail the trail, you can do that at several points. Although primarily an equestrian trail, cyclists may use the same trails always giving right-of-way to horses.

AREA INFORMATION: This area was once part of the WWII Camp Crowder Army Base. You can still see the foundations, fruit trees, open fields and other remnants of many of the hundreds of small farms purchased by the federal government for the 60,000-acre base. Camp Crowder was named for Judge Advocate General and U.S. Ambassador to Cuba Enoch H. Crowder. Thousands of soldiers went through basic training here before the camp was decommissioned in the mid-1950s, including the University of Missouri graduate Mort Walker, who immortalized the camp as Camp Swampy in his syndicated comic strip Beetle Bailey. A bronze statue in Columbia sits on the site of his favorite hangout during college.

ADDITIONAL THOUGHTS: Bicycles are permitted only on roads and trails open to vehicular traffic and horseback riding and on service roads posted closed to motorized vehicles, except when further restricted by posting.

CONTACT INFO: Missouri Department of Conservation Southwest Region Neosho Office: (417) 451-4158.

DISTANCE: 11 miles.

TERRAIN: Flat with a few rolling hills. Trails are gravel and dirt.

RIDING TIME: 2 - 3 hours.

LAND STATUS: Missouri Department of Conservation.

SERVICES & ACTIVITIES: Primitive camping. Restrooms provided.

RATING: Easy to moderate.

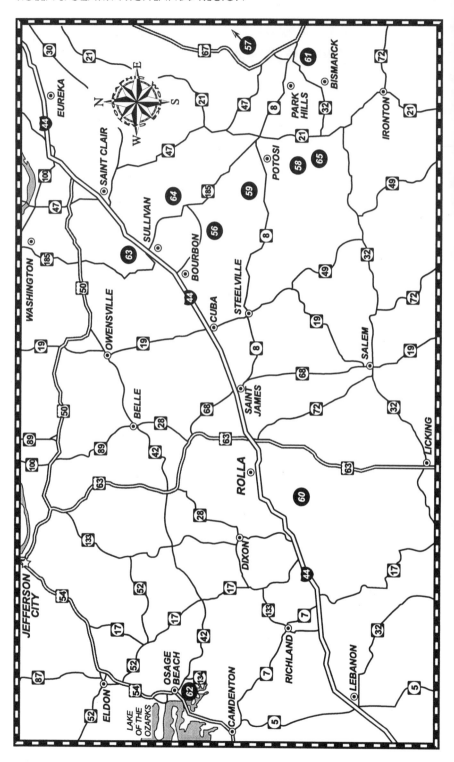

ROLLA & OZARK
HIGHLANDS REGION TRAILS

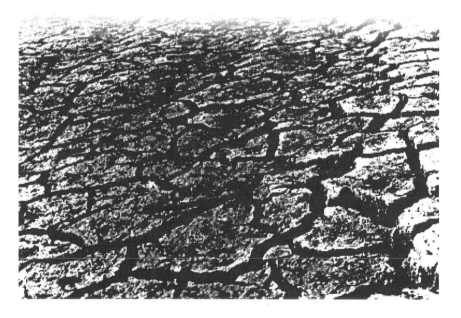

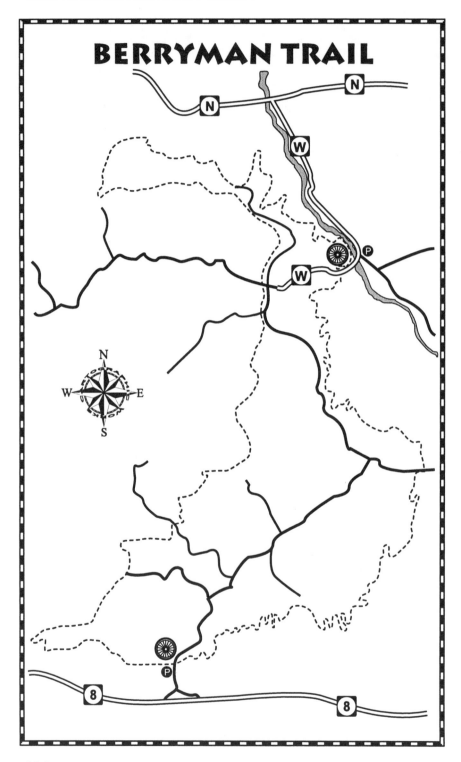

BERRYMAN TRAIL

Diana Ingram on the Berryman Trail.

56. MARK TWAIN NATIONAL FOREST

BERRYMAN TRAIL

NEAREST TOWN: Potosi (Washington County).

DIRECTIONS: Take I-44 south to Bourbon Exit 218. Take Hwy J south to Hwy N. Take Hwy N south to Hwy W, all the way to the Brazil Creek National Forest Campground on the right. Park at the campground. Or, from Potosi, take Hwy 8 west to FR 2266. From 2266 head north a few miles to the Berryman Campground.

TRAIL DESCRIPTION: Missouri mountain biking at its best. This challenging and scenic 23-mile loop of single track has well-engineered switchbacks and offers four to six hours of pedaling bliss.

Originally designed for horseback riding, now the trail is mostly single track and has no major steep climbs. However, the trail does traverse forested regions and old fields going through a variety of Ozark ecosystems. The trail also passes several Forest Service roads that can also be biked and offer alternate routes.

The Berryman hiking trail in central Missouri traverses 23 miles through a variety of scenic Ozark countryside. It winds through timbered stands of oak, pine and bottomland hardwoods—climbing switchback fashion, from low bottoms to high cherty ridges. Interesting flora and fauna abound in the old fields, glade-like rock outcroppings and deep forest. Other than occasional ATVs and motorcycles, which are only permitted on the forest service roads, mountain bikers share this trail with only equestrians, ensuring a measure of solitude. Remember to yield the right-of-way when encountering horseback riders. I found it technically challenging but not so much that it became annoyingly difficult.

HIGHLIGHTS: The scenery is wooded for most of the trail, but there are a few short sections that have been clearcut in the last twenty years. The Ozarks are a great place to ride, especially in the fall or spring.

HAZARDS: Never wanting to come home again.

AREA INFORMATION: The trail starts at Berryman Campground, the site of a Civilian Conservation Corps Camp of the same name from 1937 till the onset of World War II. The camp was jointly operated by the U.S. Army and the Forest Service and had a resident force of 300 men. Several old foundations and an old well are the only remnants of the camp itself but many roads and pine plantations in the area are enduring reminders of the good works done by these men.

ADDITIONAL THOUGHTS: Three words: guides, gear and water. Because of this trail's length, it is recommended for self-sufficient riders only. Your first time out, I highly recommend riding with an experienced group. Touring Cyclist occasionally leads guided trips here. Bring a tool kit and spare tubes. There are two springs along the trail for filtering water, so bring plenty of water or a filter and food.

CONTACT INFO: MTNF Potosi District: (314) 438-5427.

DISTANCE: 23-mile loop.

Diana Ingram and Jenny Kulier take a break at the
Brazil Creek Trailhead after a ride on the Berryman Trail.

Mile markers are located along the trail. Starting at Berryman Camp-
ground, they increase clockwise around the loop trail.
TERRAIN: Hard-packed single track with no steep climbs.
RIDING TIME: 4 - 6 hours.
LAND STATUS: Mark Twain National Forest.
SERVICES & ACTIVITIES: Food and lodging in Potosi, no water
on the trail, unless you can treat the water from the two springs.
Camping is permitted throughout the forest. The Berryman Trail
also has two car-camping trailheads.

At the Berryman Campground, there are eight campsites and
picnic tables with fire rings and restrooms. The creek is the only
water source. Berryman Campground is about one mile north of
Hwy 8, (approximately 16 miles west of Potosi or 19 miles east of
Steelville).

At the Brazil Creek Campground, there are eight campsites and
restrooms. The only water source is the creek. Brazil Creek Campground is located about six miles north of the Berryman Campground, via Forest Roads 2266 and 2265 and Hwy W, or it can be
accessed from Bourbon via Hwy N and W (approximately 17 miles).
TRAILHEAD: A popular trailhead is the Berryman Campground,
17 miles west of Potosi in Washington County. Berryman Camp is
one mile north of Highway 8 on Forest Road 2266.
RATING: Moderate.

57. MARK TWAIN NATIONAL FOREST

AUDUBON TRAIL

NEAREST TOWNS: Fredericktown, 15 miles southwest; Farmington 15 miles north.

DIRECTIONS: This trail is just south of Farmington off of Hwy 67. Take Hwy 67 south, then turn east onto Route DD at Knob Lick. Take DD to Route OO, where you go right (south) to Route T. T takes you about 5 miles to Bidwell Creek Road. Take this north 5 miles until you see the parking lot and trailhead. The trailhead is on FR 2199, a.k.a. Bidwell Creek Road.

TRAIL DESCRIPTION: Has its tough, rocky spots.

HIGHLIGHTS: This loop takes you through woods along a creek.

HAZARDS: Watch out for rocky descents.

CONTACT INFO: Mark Twain National Forest, Route 2, Hwy 72 & OO. Fredericktown, MO 63645. (573) 783-7225.

DISTANCE: 13-mile loop.

TERRAIN: Mostly flat with some hills. Hardpacked single track.

RIDING TIME: 6 - 7 hours.

LAND STATUS: Mark Twain National Forest.

SERVICES & ACTIVITIES: Camping at St. Joe State Park and Silver Mines Area.

TRAILHEAD: At parking area.

RATING: Moderate to difficult.

58. MARK TWAIN NATIONAL FOREST

COUNCIL BLUFF LAKE TRAIL

NEAREST TOWNS: Belgrade & Potosi (Iron & Washington Counties).
DIRECTIONS: From St. Louis, take Hwy 21 south through Potosi to Route C. Take C west several miles to Route DD and follow the signs. The trailhead is well marked.
TRAIL DESCRIPTION: This is a 12-mile moderate to difficult loop, with many short, steep climbs, off-camber and technical sections. Some sections—between the boat dock and the beach, and the beach to dam section—are easier. This trail has a gorgeous view of Council Bluff Lake, a well-developed trailhead and a beautiful campground. Some riders compare this favorably to the Berryman. This loop trail takes you through the Big River valley. Johnson Mountain, at 1,660 feet, provides an excellent reference point throughout your ride. A new bridge over the Big River now allows you to easily complete the loop in any weather. The first half of the trail is up and down continually sloping ridges. This is the oldest part of the trail and is hard pack, making it an excellent ride for beginners. About five miles into the ride, there's a beach and swimming area, so be sure and leave time for a dip. After the beach, the trail becomes an old double-track road that leads away from the lake, and goes up a small rocky hillside into a pine forest.
HIGHLIGHTS: Abundant wildlife and swimming at the lake.
ADDITIONAL THOUGHTS: There is a new 0.5-mile connector to the Trace Creek Section of the Ozark Trail. It is located where the trail crosses the Telleck Branch. Watch for signs. Check out nearby Johnson's Shut Ins and Elephant Rocks State Park.
CONTACT INFO: Potosi MTNF office: (314) 438-5427. Fredericktown office: (573) 783-7225.
DISTANCE: 12.5-mile loop trail.
TERRAIN: Gradual hills. Hard pack and a few rocky sections.
RIDING TIME: All afternoon.
LAND STATUS: Mark Twain National Forest.
SERVICES & ACTIVITIES: Wooded picnic area, great campground, swimming beach, boat dock and new restrooms.
TRAILHEAD: Follow the directions straight to the trailhead.
RATING: Moderate to difficult.

59. MARK TWAIN NATIONAL FOREST

MOSES AUSTIN TRAIL

NEAREST TOWN: Potosi, 15 miles west (Washington County).
DIRECTIONS: From Potosi, southwest of St. Louis, take Hwy 8 west for 11 miles. At AA go north for 3 miles, until you reach Smith Road. Go west about 1.5 miles. There is not a trailhead marker for this trail, so look for a double-track crossing on Smith Road.
TRAIL DESCRIPTION: This loop trail is comprised of rough, bulldozed fire roads, old logging roads, gravel roads and single-track paths. It includes a few technical sections. Like most Ozark terrain, this trail goes across rolling hills and over streams. This trail is considered more difficult than the Berryman, because it goes straight up and straight down hillsides rather than the more common practice of switchbacking trails to reduce erosion.

It's a terrible trail, quite honestly, since it is bulldozed for fire control, as opposed to being specifically designed for MTB'ers. Perhaps better suited for 4 wheelers. It is also not very well marked or maintained.
HIGHLIGHTS: Great views and abundant wildlife.
HAZARDS: There are several technical turns, loose rock, steep.
AREA INFORMATION: The trail gets its name from Potosi's founder. The trail is maintained by the St. Louis Council of Boy Scouts and the National Forest area is managed by the Potosi Ranger District.
CONTACT INFO: MTNF: (573) 438-5427.
DISTANCE: 14-mile loop.
TERRAIN: Moderate to difficult.
RIDING TIME: 7 hours.
LAND STATUS: Mark Twain National Forest.
TRAILHEAD: At the double-track (service road) crossing on Smith Road. No markers.
RATING: Difficult.

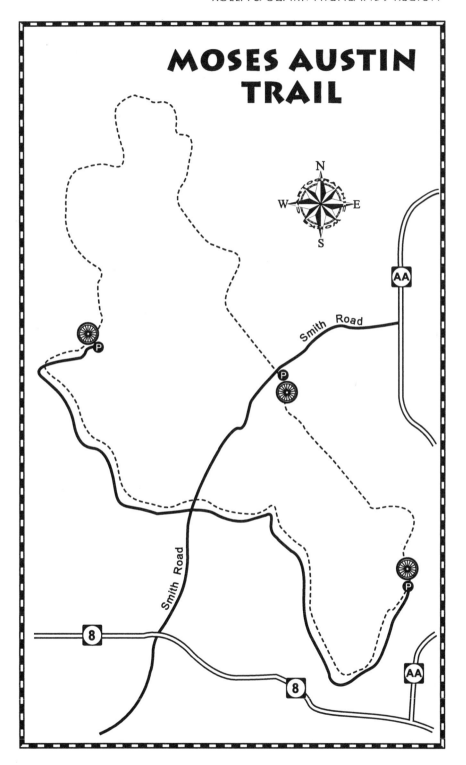

MOSES AUSTIN TRAIL

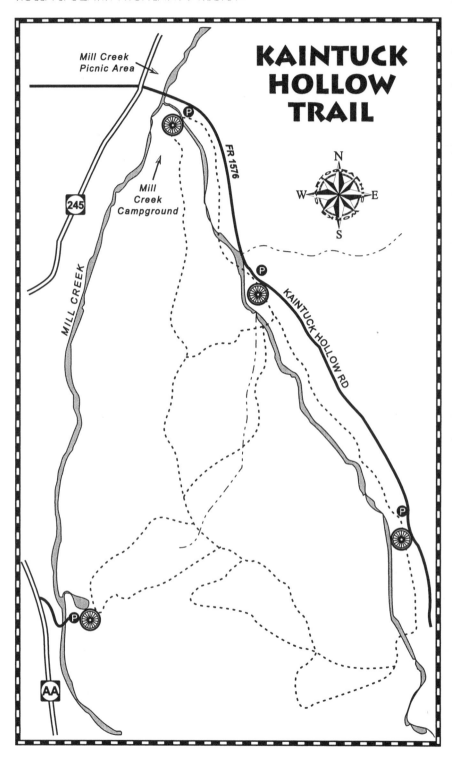

60. MARK TWAIN NATIONAL FOREST

KAINTUCK HOLLOW TRAIL

NEAREST TOWN: Rolla (Phelps County).

DIRECTIONS: From Rolla, take I-44 west approximately 5 miles to the Hwy T Exit 179 (Doolittle & Newburg). Follow Highway T south through the town of Newburg. After crossing the railroad tracks and the Little Piney Creek, immediately turn right onto Route P and travel approximately 3 miles to County Road 7550, turning left onto CR 7550. Travel approximately 2 miles until you come to the Mill Creek Picnic Area. Travel past the picnic area to the first gravel road to the left crossing Mill Creek bridge. The trail starts about 400 yards from the bridge on the right side of the road.

TRAIL DESCRIPTION: This is a multi-use trail for hiking, MTB'ing and horseback riding. This is a forested area with great scenery and some unique geological features. There are five loop trails off the main trail, allowing you to chose trail rides of one and a half to 15 miles. All trails display markers. Water is available along the trail, but is not suitable for drinking without purifying first.

HIGHLIGHTS: One trail loop goes to Wilkins Spring Pond, which has a flow of 3 million gallons of water each day. Another loop has a natural tunnel (Kaintuck Natural Bridge) 175 feet in length, adjacent to the trail.

HAZARDS: Rock outcroppings, creek crossings and a few steep sections.

AREA INFORMATION: Mill Creek Picnic Area is really nice. Good trout fishing. There is also a natural bridge here. At Big Piney River, there's canoeing and be sure and hike a bit of the Paddy Creek Wilderness Area.

ADDITIONAL THOUGHTS: While there are challenging sections, this trail is ridable for a beginner and is a great place for that not-so-graceful step of learning how to ride across creeks. Primitive camping sites (small open areas) are available near trailheads.

CONTACT INFO: Mark Twain National Forest, Houston: (417) 967-4194, or contact the Rolla District office at (573) 364-4621.
DISTANCE: 24-mile system.
TERRAIN: Moderate.
RIDING TIME: 1 - 12 hours.
LAND STATUS: Mark Twain National Forest.
SERVICES & ACTIVITIES: Water is available at Mill Creek Recreation area; five miles away, Newburg has grocers and restaurants; and Rolla is 15 miles to the east. Camping in the Kaintuck area is a unique experience. Mill Creek Picnic Area has an artesian well for drinking water, a short loop trail that features a cave, and the creek itself, which is known to many as a trophy trout stream.
TRAILHEAD: The trail starts approximately 400 yards past the Mill Creek bridge.
RATING: Moderate.

NOTES:

_____

_____

_____

_____

_____

_____

_____

_____

61. ST. JOE STATE PARK

HARRIS BRANCH TRAIL, HICKORY RIDGE TRAIL AND OTHERS

NEAREST TOWNS: Park Hills, Farmington (St. Francis County).
DIRECTIONS: From St. Louis take I-55 south to Hwy 67. Follow 67 south through Desloge. Exit onto Hwy 32 west, go a few miles, then follow the signs.
TRAIL DESCRIPTION: The Harris Branch Trail is an 11-mile loop of paved road just for bikes and hikers. The Hickory Ridge Trail can be reached from it by just blazing your way through the woods. It is easy to find. It is part of the equestrian trails, which can be accessed from Pimville Road at the parking lot. The equestrian trails are well marked. The length of maintained trails is 40 miles. There are many more miles of unofficial trails running off from the equestrian trails and the paved bike path. A 23-mile ride, winding through some of the wooded portions of the park, is provided for equestrian users. The trail forms a series of loops so riders can select a long or short ride.

HIGHLIGHTS: Great for any level of cyclist. The whole family can go and have a good time. The creek crossings are great (and sometimes very slippery). The climbs and descents are good riding.
AREA INFORMATION: St. Joe State Park—Missouri's second-largest state park—has the largest off-road-vehicle area in the Midwest, with about 1,600 acres for riding.

The park is located in the heart of the Old Lead Belt, where much of the nation's lead ore was extracted. In 1972, St. Joe Minerals Corp. ceased operations here and donated the land to the state in 1976. About 25 percent of the park land is old mined areas. The wooded portions of the 8,238-acre park provide horseback-riding and hiking trails, picnic areas and campsites and the lake has a large swimming beach.

In earlier times, the promise of riches from mining lead brought many settlers to the area, as witnessed by towns such as Rivermines, Leadington and Mineral Point. When the area's first successful mining venture began in the early 1700s, the lead was extracted from shallow pits by hand. It was not until the 1860s, after St. Joe Lead Co. was organized in New York, that the lead mining boom got its start. With the introduction of the diamond-tipped drill by St. Joe in 1869, the world's richest known deposit began to be recovered in earnest. The St. Joe Lead Corp. consolidated a number of small, independent diggings and emerged as the largest of four principal mining companies in southeast Missouri by 1900.

For more than 100 years, the "Lead Belt" of Missouri provided nearly 80 percent of the nation's mined lead. Rich new deposits of lead were discovered in 1955 in the nearby Viburnum Trend, which proved an even more significant source.

The park is a blend of oak-hickory forests natural to the area and the landscape created by the mining operation. During the mining process, the pulverized limestone, after being separated from the lead, was deposited behind a dam built across a branch of the Flat River. These sand-like tailings have all but filled the valley behind the dam. There are approximately 800 acres of these sandflats, in some places nearly 100 feet deep. After the mining ceased, the company planted prairie grasses and trees on the sandflats to stabilize the area.

These sandflats are part of a special area in the park set aside for off-road vehicles. Another result of the mining operation is four clear lakes, two of which have excellent sand beaches.

Most of the park is covered by mature second-growth forests of oak and hickory. The eastern part of the park also has several stands of native shortleaf pine. These wooded portions of the park provide excellent opportunities for hiking, picnicking and camping. The park serves as a habitat for abundant wildlife, including fox, turkey, quail and bobcat.

ADDITIONAL THOUGHTS: It is a good idea to start from one of the parking lots along the paved trail, because most of the other trails run off from it. It's a good idea to bring plenty of water, because last time I was there, the water fountains at the parking lots weren't working. It is a good idea to ride the paved bike path and the Harris Branch Loop first to get an overall feel for the area, then venture onto the unofficial trails, even if it takes up your entire first day there. You will appreciate the trails there like no others in Missouri. Also some great campgrounds for a weekend stay.

At the Missouri Mines State Historic Site on the northern edge of the park, you can check out the milling complex once used by the St. Joe Minerals Corp. The primary structures and machinery, many dating back to the 1900s, are being restored.

CONTACT INFO: St. Joe State Park, 2800 Pimville Road. Park Hills, MO 63601. (573) 431-1069

DISTANCE: 35 + mile system.

TERRAIN: Hardpack & sand flats. Vehicles tend to degrade trail.

RIDING TIME: Two hours to all weekend.

LAND STATUS: Department of Natural Resources.

SERVICES & ACTIVITIES: Water and camping, showers and laundry. Farmington, five miles east, has grocers, dining and lodging. For the convenience of horseback riders, a campground is located near the riding area. It has 35 basic sites and 15 campsites with electricity. Laundry facilities, modern restrooms, hot showers and a dumping station are located in the camping area. Sites available on a first-come basis. A designated camping area is also located along the equestrian trail.

Four clear lakes located adjacent to the tailings area offer ample opportunities for swimming and fishing. The sandlike residue from the mine has created excellent swimming beaches at Monsanto and Pim Lakes. All four lakes are stocked with bass, bluegill and channel catfish.

TRAILHEAD: Various parking lots.

RATING: Moderate to difficult.

62. LAKE OF THE OZARKS STATE PARK

TRAIL OF THE FOUR WINDS

NEAREST TOWN: Osage Beach (Camden and Miller Counties).
DIRECTIONS: Off Hwy 42 from Hwy 54.
TRAIL DESCRIPTION: 6-mile loop plus a new 9-mile extension that's a "true MTB trail"—3 or 4 good climbs with fast straight aways, many creek crossings. This is fast, true, long single track. Be prepared to share the trail with hikers and equestrians. Lake of the Ozarks State Park contains 10 trails that range in length from one-half to six miles. Trails lead through dense oak-hickory forests and lush ravines, across open sunny glades and along towering bluffs overlooking the lake. In addition to hiking and backpacking trails, two equestrian trails wind through the east end of the park. Trail rides are offered for a nominal charge at the park stables. Trail information is available at the trail center, or while in Osage Beach, stop by Ozark Bicycles across from the KFC, near Junction 54 & 42.
HAZARDS: Watch for blue-hairs wandering the woods looking for the outlet malls.
AREA INFORMATION: Enjoy the solitude of an undeveloped cove, hidden along the shorelines of one of Missouri's largest lakes. Swim, fish, boat, or simply take in the view from a shady campsite overlooking the Lake of the Ozarks. The 17,203-acre Lake of the Ozarks State Park offers the opportunity to enjoy all the varied recreational activities on the lake, plus much more.

Located in the Osage River Hills, the park contains many natural features typical of the Ozark region, ranging from rugged, wooded areas to delicate cave formations. The hills and ridges are covered with dense oak-hickory forests, dotted with sunny, rocky openings called glades. Plants and animals such as the Indian paintbrush, Missouri evening primrose, six-lined racerunner and fence lizard have adapted to the glades' shallow soils and dry conditions.

Lake of the Ozarks State Park was originally established by the National Park Service in the mid-1930s, following the damming of the Osage River and the creation of the lake. The recreational area was turned over to the state in 1946. Lake of the Ozarks State Park, the largest in the state park system, is administered by the Missouri Department of Natural Resources.

Wild turkeys, great blue heron, deer, fox, raccoon, owls, and in the winter, bald eagles are among the wildlife making their homes in the forested hills surrounding the lake.

During the summer months, the park naturalist leads guided nature hikes and presents evening nature programs. Check at the park office for information on the location and times for the programs and guided hikes.

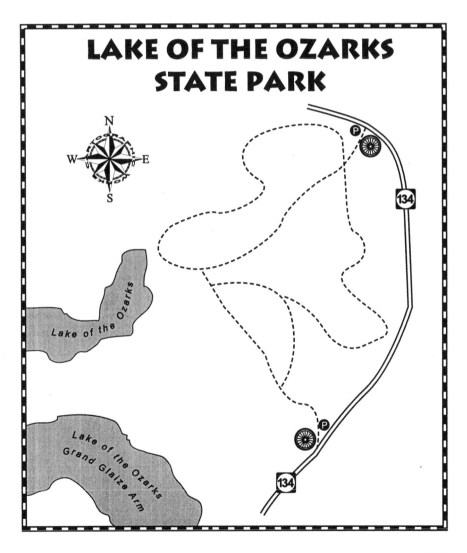

LAKE OF THE OZARKS
STATE PARK

The 1,275-acre Patterson Hollow Wild Area gives visitors a chance for solitude in a wilderness setting. Woodland Trail offers access to the wild area.

ADDITIONAL THOUGHTS: Ozark Caverns, located in the south end of the park, is best known for its unusual "Angels' Showers," a formation of stalactites and waterfalls. For a nominal fee, guided educational tours are given on a daily basis during the summer. Because of its high-quality natural features, the area surrounding Ozark Caverns has been designated as a state natural area, and includes spring-fed streams, seeps, caves, fens, glades and deep valleys. A self-guiding trail takes visitors through this special area.

CONTACT INFO: Park Office, Lake of the Ozarks State Park, Kaiser, MO 65047. (314) 348-2694. Ozark Caverns: (314) 346-2500.

DISTANCE: 6-mile loop around lake.

TERRAIN: Fairly moderate. Partly hilly.

RIDING TIME: 3 hours.

LAND STATUS: Department of Natural Resources.

SERVICES & ACTIVITIES: Cabins and camping, boating, fishing, swimming, horseback riding, picnicking. Approximately 230 tent and trailer campsites, both basic and improved, are available year-round. Facilities available in the camping area include modern restrooms, laundry facilities, dumping stations and a store. Four organized group camps are available.

Eight primitive log cabins are available year-round for campers who want a rustic experience without pitching a tent. Each cabin offers a quiet secluded setting with a picturesque view. Cabins are furnished with wood-burning stove, table and chairs, three double beds and barbecue grill. Area facilities include a central showerhouse/restroom and swimming area. Reservations may be made at the park office.

There are two free swimming beaches with bathhouses and shady picnic areas nearby. Boats can be rented either for fishing or skiing, and nearby park stores sell supplies such as tackle and gas.

TRAILHEAD: At parking area.

RATING: Moderate.

63. LONG RIDGE CONSERVATION AREA

EQUESTRIAN TRAIL

NEAREST TOWN: Sullivan (Franklin County).

DIRECTIONS: From Sullivan, take Route AF north for 3 miles to Ridge Road, continue north for 1 mile to the parking lot on the left. A second trailhead is 2 miles farther down Ridge Road.

TRAIL DESCRIPTION: This nine-mile trail winds through this long, skinny 1,816-acre area. The area is vaguely shaped like a north-south barbell, with loop trails at either ends. All along the eastern side of the area is Ridge Road, in case you need to bail from the trail.

HAZARDS: Horse trails are open to equestrians and mountain bikers only from December 31 through October 15. Although primarily an equestrian trail, cyclists may use the same trails always giving right-of-way to horses.

AREA INFORMATION: This area includes two dry sinkholes. Ecosystems include post oak woodland savanna and chert savanna. This has only been a conservation area since 1995.

ADDITIONAL THOUGHTS: Bicycles are permitted only on roads and trails open to vehicular traffic and horseback riding and on service roads posted closed to motorized vehicles, except when further restricted by posting.

CONTACT INFO: Missouri Department of Conservation East Central Region Sullivan Office: (573) 468-3335.

DISTANCE: 9 miles of seasonal, developed trail.

TERRAIN: Typical Ozark terrain. The trail is predominantly dirt and grass. Upland oak and hickory forest. Varies from one end to the other in steepness. The southern end is post oak flats (flat woods savanna) and the northern end has steeper terrain and much deeper draws. Most of the trail is less than 7 percent grade, with just a few steeper places. Trail runs adjacent to Spring Creek but doesn't cross it, so the trail remains high and dry.

RIDING TIME: 2 - 3 hours.

LAND STATUS: Missouri Department of Conservation.

SERVICES & ACTIVITIES: Primitive camping allowed in designated areas only. No restrooms or water sources.

TRAILHEAD: Several trailheads along Ridge Road.

RATING: Easy to moderate.

64. MERAMEC CONSERVATION AREA

EQUESTRIAN TRAIL

NEAREST TOWN: Sullivan (Franklin County).

DIRECTIONS: From Sullivan, take Hwy 185 south for 4.5 miles to entrance on left. Follow gravel road for 1.5 miles to parking lot.

TRAIL DESCRIPTION: This trail loops and meanders throughout this 3,879-acre area. The area is approximately bordered on the west by the Meramec River, on the south by Hwy 185, on the west by Route K. The terrain is rolling hills, constantly heading up and down approximately 200 feet of relief, from 700 to 900 feet of elevation. Although primarily an equestrian trail, cyclists may use the same trails always giving right-of-way to horses.

HAZARDS: This trail is closed during the spring turkey season and the fall firearms deer season.

AREA INFORMATION: Much of the 3,879-acre parcel was purchased by the state between 1925 and 1930. Sheer cliffs along the Meramec River form the western border of the area, affording a scenic view of the river valley and surrounding hills. The area contains six caves, a great blue heron rookery, abundant wildlife and varying forest types. Other attractions include the town of Reedville, a former CCC camp, Lone Hill Lookout Tower and old mines.

ADDITIONAL THOUGHTS: Bicycles are permitted only on roads and trails open to vehicular traffic and horseback riding and on service roads posted closed to motorized vehicles, except when further restricted by posting.

CONTACT INFO: MDOC Sullivan Office: (573) 468-3335.

DISTANCE: 12 miles.

TERRAIN: Varies from hard pack, to grassy and rocky sections.

RIDING TIME: 2 - 3 hours.

LAND STATUS: Missouri Department of Conservation.

SERVICES & ACTIVITIES: No camping or water. Camping is available at the nearby Meramec State Park. Also, this area fronts 4.8 miles of the Meramec River, so bring your fishing pole. In addition to the 12 miles of horse trails here, there are eight miles of foot trail, and a great 1.5-mile paved trail suitable for wheelchairs.

RATING: Moderate.

65. MARK TWAIN NATIONAL FOREST

RED BLUFF

NEAREST TOWN: Caledonia (Washington County).
DIRECTIONS: From Salem, take Hwy 32 east for 54 miles to Hwy 21. Go north on Hwy 21 to Route C, then go west. Where it forks, watch for signs to Red Bluff. Or, from Potosi, take Hwy 21 south for 12 miles, then go north on Route C.
TRAIL DESCRIPTION: A moderate 1-mile loop trail that runs along the creek.
HIGHLIGHTS: Abundant wildlife. Creek adds a nice scenic touch to this ride.
HAZARDS: Not many. Watch for high water.
AREA INFORMATION: In the middle of *nowhere.*
CONTACT INFO: Contact the Potosi MTNF office at (573) 438-5427 or the Fredericktown office at (573) 783-7225.
DISTANCE: 1 mile trail.
TERRAIN: Moderately flat with a few rolling hills.
RIDING TIME: All afternoon.
LAND STATUS: Mark Twain National Forest.
SERVICES & ACTIVITIES: Hiking, biking and horse use. No developed facilities along trail. Bring your own drinking water. Primitive camping is allowed.
TRAILHEAD: At parking area.
RATING: Moderate.

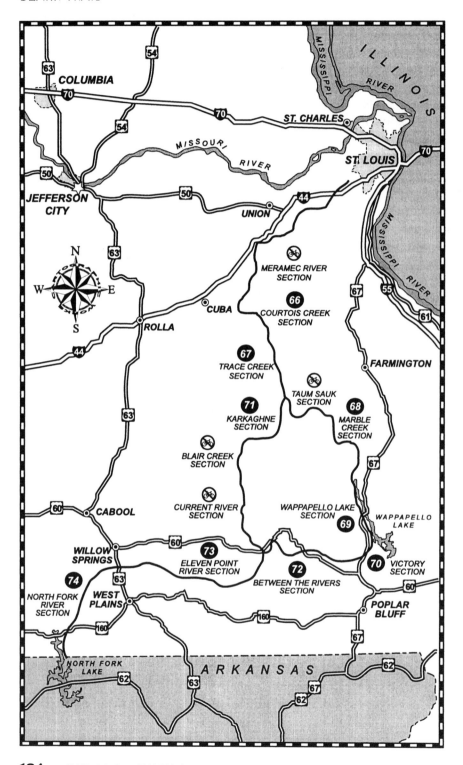

OZARK TRAIL

When completed the Ozark Trail will connect more than 700 miles of hiking and biking trails in Missouri and Arkansas. As of the fall of 1998, a total of 307.5 miles of the Ozark Trail are complete. Only the sections highlighted in this book permit mountain biking.

OT SECTIONS THAT PERMIT MOUNTAIN BIKING:

NORTHERN REGION

EASTERN REGION

WESTERN REGION

SOUTHERN REGION

MAP NOTES: The numbered sections on the opposite page are open for mountain biking. The unnumbered sections of the Ozark Trail are closed to cycling, but hikers are welcome. Additionally, the map highlights the proposed trail in its entirety. Not all sections are completed. For brochures on many sections of the trail, call the Department of Natural Resources at 1 (800) 334-6946.

Ozark
Trail

INTRODUCTION
TO THE OZARK TRAIL

The Ozark Trail is like the Katy Trail on steroids. Whereas the Katy Trail is flat, straight and takes you through the Missouri River Valley, the Ozark Trail is anything but flat and straight. It blends all of the things that make the Ozarks so unique and inviting: forested, green rolling hills out to the horizon, clear Ozark streams, exposed granite and limestone relief, glades, waterfalls and utter seclusion. The constantly changing relief of steep southern creek drainages makes this the perfect place to ride and soak in how gorgeous southern Missouri can be.

Not all of the OT sections are open to MTB, but who cares!?! The sections that are open offer several lifetimes of unforgettable single track. If I could find a place down there to plug in my lap top I'd never come home.

The trail is envisioned to someday extend from St. Louis through the scenic Ozarks to the Arkansas border where it will connect with the Arkansas Ozark Highlands Trail and proceed west to the Arkansas-Oklahoma border.

Help make this proposal a reality by volunteering to do trail maintenance or construction, by supporting the agencies involved in trail management or by making monetary contributions specifically earmarked for Ozark Trail development.

ADDITIONAL THOUGHTS: The official Ozark Trail marker is a white 4-by-6-inch rectangle with a green symbol. Two tilted markers placed one above the other warn of an abrupt turn in the trail in the direction of the tilt. Painted blazes are also used to identify the route. Always carry a map and compass.

LAND STATUS: The development of the Ozark Trail is an ambitious project that has been undertaken by the members of the Ozark Trail Council, which includes state and federal land-managing agencies, trail groups and landowners.

MAPS: Most of these OT sections are highlighted in various free DNR brochures, including topos and highways. If you just have to spend money to make it feel like vacation, you can also order the various USGS maps detailed on each of the following trail sections.

CONTACT INFO: If you would like more specific information on this trail, write to the Ozark Trail Coordinator, c/o Missouri Department of Natural Resources, P.O. Box 176, Jefferson City, MO 65102, or call 1 (800) 334-6946. Since this is a multi-agency effort, below is a comprehensive list of agencies that develop and maintain different portions of the Ozark Trail.

Mo. Department of Natural Resources
Ozark Trail Coordinator
P.O. Box 176
Jefferson City, MO 65102
(800) 334-6946

Missouri Department of Conservation
Natural History Section
P.O. Box 180
Jefferson City, MO 65102
(573) 751-4115

Mark Twain National Forest
401 Fairgrounds Road
Rolla, MO 65401
(573) 364-4621

Ozark National Scenic Riverways
P.O. Box 490
Van Buren, MO 63965
(573) 323-4236

U.S. Army Corps of Engineers
HC 2, Box 2349
Wappapello, MO 63966
(573) 222-8562

For volunteer information, contact:
Niki Aberle
OT Volunteer Coordinator
(573) 634-2322

For Ozark Highlands Trail info, contact:
Ozark Highlands Trail Association
Tim Ernst
411 Patricia Lane
Fayetteville, AR 72703
(501) 442-2799 / Fax: (501) 442-3940
E-mail: OHTA@ArkansasUSA.com

Arkansas Trails Council
One Capital Mall
Little Rock, AR 72201

"NAZ"
AND THE CENTRAL
OZARK TRAIL NETWORK

By Jennifer Kulier
Associate Editor, *Cycle St. Louis*

Mountain bikers have a friend in the Mark Twain National Forest and his name is Paul Nazarenko. "Naz," a recreation specialist at the U.S. Forest Service's Potosi Ranger Station, has a vision for creating a linked network of trails in his beautiful corner of the world, and he thinks mountain bikers are the key to making this trail system work.

"Trails are only a small part of my job, but this year I decided to spend the time to get this trail network in place," said Nazarenko. "Seeing the increased use of the Berryman among mountain bikers in the last couple years, I'm hoping they will help with trail construction, and then use and help maintain the trails."

To get the trails built, open and in good repair, Naz needs the support of mountain bikers who are willing to help him with physical work like brush clearing. But perhaps the most important way to see that awesome trails remain a priority is to use them, and when you do, let the U.S. Forest Service know you appreciate them. You can contact the USFS-Potosi Ranger District and Paul Nazarenko at Hwy 8 West, P.O. Box 188, Potosi, MO. 63664. (573) 438-5427.

SIDETRIP:
TAUM SAUK MOUNTAIN & JOHNSON'S SHUT-INS

This 33-mile section isn't open to cyclists but, if you're in the area, it's worth checking out. Taum Sauk Mountain is the highest point in the state (bring your Everest oxygen mask) and this area offers great hiking and camping.

The Taum Sauk OT Section is one of the most scenic and rugged sections along the entire Ozark Trail. It passes through the Bell Mountain Wilderness Area, Johnson's Shut-Ins and Taum Sauk Mountain State Parks. Taum Sauk Mountain is the highest point in Missouri at 1,772 feet (Arkansas' highest point is 2,750 feet in comparison). It also passes through the Proffit and Ketcherside Mountain Conservation Areas.

To get to this OT section, the western access is located on Hwy A, three miles north of the intersection with Hwy 49 at Edgehill in Iron County. There is a small U.S. Forest Service parking lot on the east side of Hwy A. Access to the OT trail section midpoint is at Johnson's Shut-Ins State Park located off Hwy N in Reynolds County. For the eastern access to the OT section, or to check out Taum Sauk Mountain State Park, go to the end of Hwy CC or the parking area on the west side of Hwy 21 just north of Royal Gorge.

Both Johnson's Shut-Ins and Taum Sauk Mountain State Parks have developed camping areas. The three-mile looped Mina Sauk Falls Trail is a personal favorite. It is accessible from the Taum Sauk parking lot. The views of rolling hills rival the Blue Ridge Mountains. At Johnson's Shut-Ins there's also great swimming. It may be crowded because the Black River Shut-Ins are a popular swimming hole.

For more information, contact Taum Sauk Mountain State Park in Ironton and Johnson's Shut-Ins State Park in Middlebrook. Same phone: (573) 546-2450. Or, request a brochure from DNR, P.O. Box 176, Jefferson City, MO 65102. Or call 1 (800) 334-6946. Information is online too. Do a search on Missouri state parks.

66. OT

COURTOIS CREEK SECTION

NEAREST TOWNS: Sullivan, Steelville (Crawford, Franklin and Washington Counties).
DIRECTIONS: Courtois Creek's southern trailhead is at Hazel Creek Campground, a short distance off Route Z on a dirt road. Proceed northwest to FR 2247 to Berryman Campground and Trail (bordered by FR 2266) and onto FR 2265 after Hwy W intersects; there the trail deadends. The trail connection to Huzzah Conservation Area is not completed. Mountain biking IS NOT permitted on the Ozark Trail as it passes through the Huzzah Conservation Area, nor anywhere else within the Huzzah Conservation Area.

But since you're down here, put on the hiking boots and check it out. Huzzah Conservation Area can be reached by taking I-44 to Cuba (Exit 208), then turn south on Hwy 19 and go to Steelville (8 miles). Continue 6 miles east on Hwy 8 to the junction of Hwy E, go north on E 6 miles to Huzzah Conservation Area. Hwys D, N, H and E all offer access to various points along this section.
TRAIL DESCRIPTION: Pronounced locally as Cord-o-way, the northern part of this section of the OT has yet to be completed, but it does have some pedalable trail. This OT section is basically the western half of the Berryman Trail. The proposed length would extend from the southern boundary of Onondaga State Park and go through the Huzzah Conservation Area.

The southern end of this section is open, and utilizes the western section of the Berryman Trail. By possibly the end of 1998, it will connect to the Trace Creek section (across Hwy 8) and the Hazel Creek Campground portion will be completed.

The completed section runs from Hazel Creek Campground to Forest Road 2247 to Hwy 8, then west to Forest Road 2266 which joins the Berryman Trail. The connection from the northwest portion of the Berryman Trail to Huzzah Conservation Area has not been completed.
HIGHLIGHTS: Views of the Meramec River and Courtois Creek.
HAZARDS: Note the low-water crossing across Courtois Creek is impassable when the waters are high. Be aware that the Berryman is also a prime equine trail that is sometimes used for organized equine trail races.

AREA INFORMATION: This trail passes by the confluence of the Meramec River and the Huzzah and Courtois Creeks.

CONTACT INFO: MTNF Potosi Ranger District: (573) 438-5427. Meramec State Park: (573) 468-6072. Cabin and canoe reservations: (314) 468-6519. Huzzah Conservation Area contact: Missouri Department of Conservation, P.O. Box 180, Jefferson City, MO 65102. Phone (573) 751-4115.

DISTANCE: 6 miles.

TERRAIN: Switchbacks, valley slopes and bluffs.

RIDING TIME: 2 hours.

LAND STATUS: This OT section is managed by the U.S. Forest Service's Mark Twain National Forest Potosi Ranger District. Huzzah Conservation Area is managed by the Department of Conservation.

SERVICES & ACTIVITIES: There is primitive camping in the MTNF at the Brazil and Hazel Creek areas. There is also developed camping in Onondaga State Park across the Meramec River. Huzzah Conservation Area has primitive camping. There is also camping at Meramec State Park.

Huzzah Conservation Area has 20 caves and a high-ground panoramic scenic view of the Huzzah Valley. Also within this local area are canoe rental, river access facilities, beach, and access to the confluence of the two main creeks and the Meramec River.

Hiking, swimming, canoeing, fishing, tubing and boating are all popular sports along the Meramec River and its tributaries.

TRAILHEAD: Courtois Creek's southern trailhead is at Hazel Creek Campground. Hwys D, N, H and E all offer access to various points along this section.

RATING: Moderate to difficult.

MAPS: No freely distributed maps of this section currently exist. If you are looking for topos, contact the MTNF's Potosi Ranger District or consult the Missouri Department of Conservation's Atlas for the Crawford County map. The Meramec River forms the northwest quadrant borders of Huzzah Conservation Area and the Huzzah and Courtois Creeks flow into the southwestern boundary. Maps of Franklin and Washington Counties are also in the Atlas. For USGS maps, request the Berryman, Courtois and Huzzah sections.

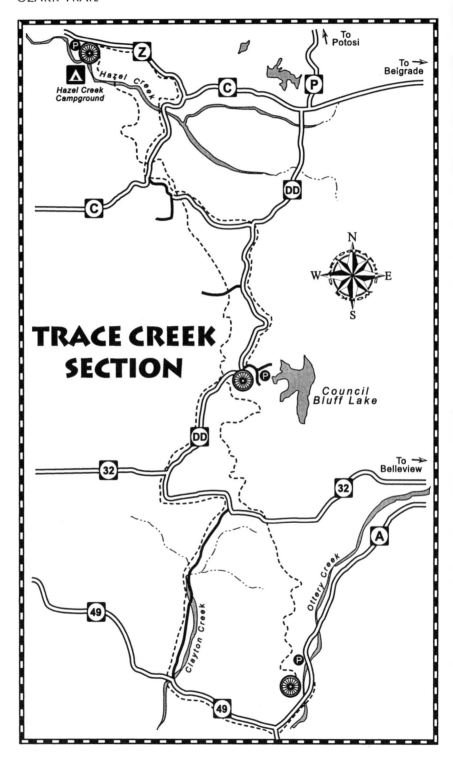

TRACE CREEK SECTION

67. OT
TRACE CREEK SECTION

NEAREST TOWNS: West of Belgrade, near Potosi, Belleview, Courtois, Viburnum and Black (Iron & Washington Counties).

DIRECTIONS: To get to the northern trailhead, from Potosi, head southwest on Route P turn west on Route C, then take Route Z north (right) to FR 2408. Turn west (left) and go several miles to the parking lot. For the southern trailhead, from Black, go north on Hwy 49 about 4 miles, turning right (east) onto Route A. Drive a short distance and look for the parking lot and sign on your left.

TRAIL DESCRIPTION: Open to MTB'ing, hiking and horses.

HIGHLIGHTS: This trail combines clear Ozark streams, dry granite barrens, panoramic mountaintop views and deep forests that filter the summer sun.

HAZARDS: Poison ivy, fairly remote location.

AREA INFORMATION: The trail's northern entry point is located at Hazel Creek Campground. From that point, it proceeds south following a continually changing landscape that leads MTB'ers through dense oak, hickory and pine forests, into shaded hollows and across windswept ridge tops. It crosses several small tributaries and Hazel Creek, which is a major permanently flowing creek. It also crosses several state highways including 32, C, DD, but these crossings are difficult to detect from the highways before ending at Highway A. An older section was built in 1968 and a five-mile addition was constructed in 1983.

DISTANCE: 24 miles.

TERRAIN: Hardpack, exposed roots and some moderately technical sections.

RIDING TIME: All day.

LAND STATUS: Potosi Forest Ranger District of the Mark Twain National Forest.

SERVICES & ACTIVITIES: Facilities (Hazel Creek) restrooms, camping and picnicking.

TRAILHEAD: The Hazel Creek Campground at the southern terminus of the Courtois Creek section just off Hwy Z is the northern trailhead. The southern trailhead is at Ottery Creek on Hwy A near the intersection with Hwy 49, four miles north of Black.

RATING: Moderate.

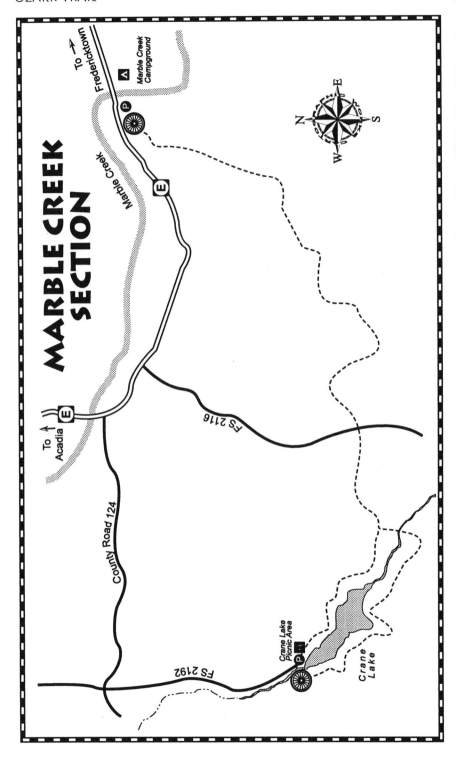

68. OT

MARBLE CREEK SECTION

NEAREST TOWNS: Ironton and Fredericktown (Madison & Iron Counties).

DIRECTIONS: The eastern trailhead can be accessed at Marble Creek Campground off Hwy E at Forest Road 2520 several miles west of where the St. Francois River crosses the highway and just over the Madison county line after leaving Iron County.

From Ironton go 2 miles south on Hwy 21, east on Hwy E 12 miles to Marble Creek Recreation Area. From Fredericktown, take Hwy E 18 miles west to Marble Creek. Park at the trailhead. Trail begins just across from Hwy E.

The western trailhead is at Crane Lake, 12.2 miles south of Ironton on Hwy 21. To start there, go east on the gravel road at Chloride and go 3.2 miles to a county road, turn south and go 1.9 miles. From Fredericktown, head 18 miles east on Hwy E to county road, 2.8 miles to county road south and go 1.9 miles to the lake.

TRAIL DESCRIPTION: This is Ozark riding at its best. This trail skirts the sides of 1,000-foot hills, and is a single-track roller coaster ride on rocky ground. This 8-mile-long section, which will eventually extend 21 miles, will connect the Taum Sauk section to the west and the St. Francois River section of the eastern loop of the Ozark Trail in the Fredericktown Ranger district to the south. In addition to the Ozark Trail, there are also several Jeep trails so be sure to pick up a topo map at the campground.

The current northwestern access point is at Crane Lake, the middle (currently the end) portion trailhead is at Marble Creek, and the eventual southern trailhead is at Sam A. Baker State Park. This is also a foot and horse trail that crosses Forest Road 2116 and Minimum Road that intersects E to the north.

HIGHLIGHTS: This area of Marble Creek rushes for 20 miles through the ruggedest St. Francis Mountains. Gorgeous.

AREA INFORMATION: Marble Creek is named for the colored dolomite here, which was mined for use in buildings as "Taum Sauk Marble." An old grist-mill dam still visible today was the third to be built here and it operated until 1935. It was made of stone and concrete reinforced with iron wagon-wheel hoops.

CONTACT INFO: Mark Twain National Forest Fredericktown Ranger District, Route 2, Box 175, Fredericktown, MO 63645. (573) 783-7225.

DISTANCE: 8 miles. Will eventually extend 21 miles.

TERRAIN: Rocky and hilly.

RIDING TIME: 2 - 3 hours.

LAND STATUS: Mark Twain National Forest.

SERVICES & ACTIVITIES: At Marble Creek Recreation Area, there is camping, picnicking, restrooms and water. At Crane Lake, there is a picnic table and restrooms, but overnight camping is not allowed. Both areas also allow horseback riding.

TRAILHEAD: Marble Creek Campground & Crane Lake.

RATING: Moderate to difficult.

MAPS: Call the U.S. Forest Service and request the Salem-Potosi Map, $3. Potosi-Fredericktown Ranger District: (573) 438-5427. USGS quad map Iron county 7.5 minute series (modified for the U.S. Forest Service) shows this portion of the Ozark Trail clearly.

NOTES:

_____

_____

_____

_____

_____

_____

_____

_____

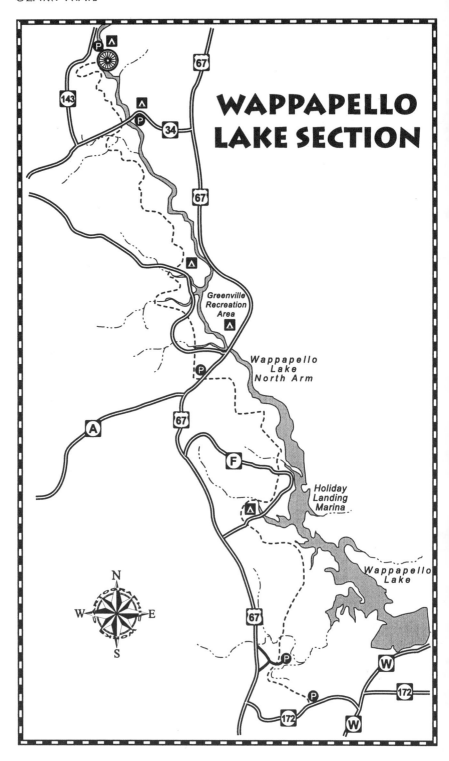

WAPPAPELLO LAKE SECTION

69. OT

WAPPAPELLO LAKE SECTION

NEAREST TOWN: Poplar Bluff (Wayne and Butler Counties).
DIRECTIONS: The northern trailhead is 1 mile south of Sam A. Baker State Park on Hwy 143. The trail can also be accessed from the campground in Sam A. Baker State Park.

The southern trailhead is the north spur connecting the long Wappapello Lake Trail to the Ozark Trail or the trailhead with parking on Hwy 172 at the park.
TRAIL DESCRIPTION: This 38-mile OT section extends from near the Sam A. Baker State Park to Hwy 172. A spur trail links Lake Wappapello State Park to the Ozark Trail.
AREA INFORMATION: This trail passes through the 1,300-foot St. Francois Mountains, Big Creek Valley and Creek, Green Mountain and Logan Creek Valley at Sam A. Baker State Park. It also passes through the 1,854-acre Lake Wappapello State Park and oak-hickory forests on the Allison Peninsula.
CONTACT INFO: U.S. Army Corps of Engineers, St. Louis District Project Office: (573) 222-8562. Or write: Project Manager, Wappapello Lake Project office, HC 2, Box 2349, Wappapello, MO 63966. The Wappapello Information Hotline is (573) 222-8139. Wappapello cabin rentals (April 1 - October 31) is (636) 297-3247.
DISTANCE: 38 miles.
TERRAIN: Varies from flat to hilly to several steep climbs.
RIDING TIME: All day.
LAND STATUS: Department of Natural Resources.
SERVICES & ACTIVITIES: At Baker, there's a lodge and hiking in the 4,180-acre wild area. At Lake Wappapello, there's shelters, swimming, horse and hiking trails, primitive camping and cabins.
TRAILHEAD: At parking lot near campground.
RATING: Difficult.
MAPS: From DNR, request "Baker Trail and Wild Area Guide" and "Lake Wappapello Trail Map" and the "Lake Wappapello State Park." The Corps of Engineers St. Louis District's color map "Wappapello Lake, Missouri," shows the entire trail region.

70. OT

VICTORY SECTION
AKA BRUSHY CREEK TRAIL

NEAREST TOWNS: Poplar Bluff, Ellsinore (Butler, Carter and Wayne Counties).

DIRECTIONS: This trail stretches from just north of Ellsinore to Wappapello Lake State Park, northeast of Poplar Bluff, entirely within the Mark Twain National Forest. At the present time, 24 miles of this section, which will eventually total approximately 30 miles, are open to public use. This section will run from Hwy 172 to Ellsinore. Parking is currently available at Route F, Hwy 172, Wrangler, Upalika Pond and Brush Arbor trailheads. The trail is open to MTB'ing, hiking and horse riders.

Detailed directions for reaching the six Victory trailheads from Poplar Bluffs are from the "Mark Twain National Forest" brochure. For the Hwy 172 trailhead (parking available), go 16 miles north on Hwy 67, then 1 mile east on Hwy 172. For Wrangler (parking available), go 4 miles north on Hwy 67, 1 mile north on BC 402, 4 miles west on FR 3110. For Upalika Pond (parking available), go 9 miles north on Hwy 67, 1 mile north on BC 402, 6 miles west on FR 3110, 5 miles west on FR 3112. For Brush Arbor, go 7 miles north on Hwy 67, 11 miles west on Hwy 60, 2 miles east on BC 415, 3 miles north on BC 417. For Victory School, go 7 miles north on Hwy 67, 2 miles west on Hwy 60, 1 mile north on BC 410.

TRAIL DESCRIPTION: Currently 24 of 30 planned trail miles (DNR brochure), or 37 miles ("Mark Twain National Forest" U.S. Forest Service brochure), are open to public use for mountain biking, hiking and equestrian use. Note the 8-mile equestrian trail extension (near the eastern end) is a southern loop with a spur ending at the Victory Horse Trail trailhead near Cane Creek.

The eastern Victory section trailhead is at Hwy 172 and the western end at Ellsinore, at the intersection of Hwys V, N, DD and A. The section crosses Brushy Creek on its way to merge with the Black River to the east. Victory Horse Trail extends south of the Victory section of the Ozark Trail.

There are multiple ways to find this trail. The system lies just west of Hwy 67 and north of Hwy 60. County Road 410 will take you to Victory trailhead; Hwy A just north of Ellsinore has another trailhead. This trail starts out as a long uphill climb and turns into a roller coaster ride of uphills and downhills. It is characterized by rocky washout descents and wide single track. There are a few small creek watercrossings. The trail surface alternates from bare clay and rock to leaf and pine needle covered. It is easy to lose your way off this trail. While it is marked with the gray diamond symbols similar to other parts of the Ozark Trail, many intersecting forest roads, old logging roads and other trails make it sometimes difficult to follow.

HIGHLIGHTS: The downhills, of course.

HAZARDS: Watch for high water at crossings.

ADDITIONAL THOUGHTS: Spring and fall are great times to ride this one. This trail would best be ridden in the early Spring or late Fall due to overgrowth, poison oak and poison ivy. If you are looking for a quieter trail that will give your granny gear a workout, this trail is it.

CONTACT INFO: MTNF Poplar Bluff (573) 785-1475.

DISTANCE: 24 miles.

TERRAIN: Hilly.

RIDING TIME: All day.

LAND STATUS: MTNF Poplar Ranger District.

SERVICES & ACTIVITIES: Poplar Bluff, Greenville and little Ellsinore have plenty of food and lodging. There's no water along the trail itself. Parking is available at Route F, Hwy 172, Wrangler, Upalika Pond and Brush Arbor trailheads. See table on p.11 of the "Mark Twain National Forest" brochure for trailhead facilities that include fishing (Upalika), hiking (all), picnicking (all), trailer space and horseback trails (all). There are no swimming, sanitary facilities or drinking water so be forewarned! Accommodations for combined uses including horseback riders.

TRAILHEAD: The Victory Trail section has six access points.

RATING: Moderate to challenging.

MAPS: DNR's "Victory Section" brochure.

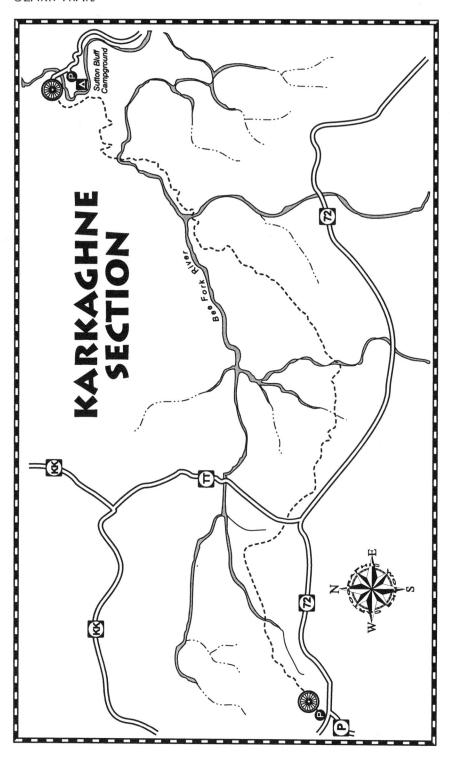

71. OT

KARKAGHNE SECTION

NEAREST TOWNS: Southeastern trailhead near Centerville. Western trailhead near Bunker (Reynolds County).

DIRECTIONS: Take Hwy 21 north out of Centerville to reach FR 2233. The trail starts at Sutton Bluff Trailhead. Sutton Bluff Recreation Area access point is reached by going 3-4 miles on Hwy 21 northwest of Centerville; 7 miles southwest on Forest Road 2221, 3 miles south on Forest Road 2236. The south trailhead on Hwy 72 is at the intersection with Hwy P near Bunker.

TRAIL DESCRIPTION: The Karkaghne section is a 15-mile-long ridge-top trail traveling from 800 feet to about 1,200 feet along the Bee Fork Creek drainage, passing through Grasshopper Hollow and within hiking distance of several pioneer cemeteries. In the future, it will connect the Trace Creek section to the north and currently connects to the Blair Creek Section in the south. The current northern access point is at Sutton Bluff Campground, and the southern trailhead is on Hwy P.

HIGHLIGHTS: Gorgeous views and pioneer cemeteries. Sutton Bluff area is near the Huzzah River and Spring Creek. Great floating streams, with several canoe rentals nearby.

HAZARDS: Watch for slippery steep sections and fallen trees. This trail is used heavily by equestrians, so be ready to yield trail.

AREA INFORMATION: Brushy Creek Resort is east on Hwy J.

ADDITIONAL THOUGHTS: Steep climbs and lots of deadfall may make you wish you had traded your bike for your hiking boots.

CONTACT INFO: Salem Ranger District, U.S. Forest Service: (573) 729-6656. Or call the Potosi Ranger District at (573) 438-5427.

DISTANCE: 12 miles one-way.

TERRAIN: Moderately hilly to steep and technical.

RIDING TIME: 4 - 6 hours.

LAND STATUS: MTNF Potosi & Salem Ranger Districts.

SERVICES & ACTIVITIES: At Sutton Bluff are 35 campsites, restrooms and water. There's also fishing, hiking & picnic tables.

TRAILHEAD: Present access points are at Hwy 72, Hwy TT and Sutton Bluff Campground.

RATING: Moderate to difficult.

MAPS: Request free OT maps from DNR. The Salem Ranger District sells district maps for $3. Call (573) 729-6656.

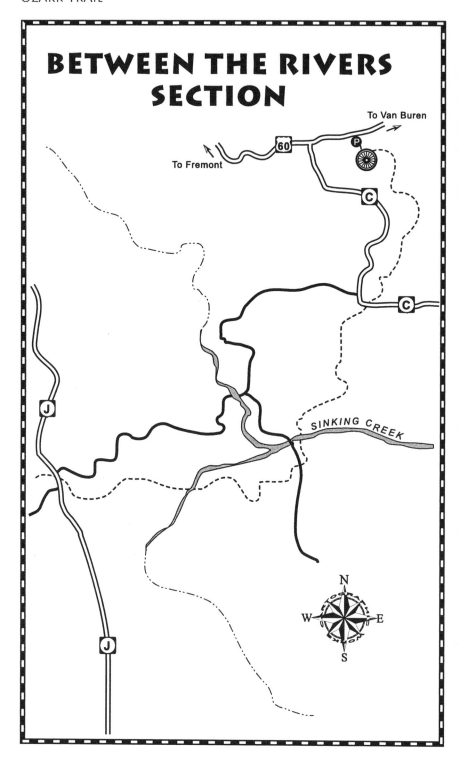

BETWEEN THE RIVERS SECTION

To Van Buren

To Fremont

SINKING CREEK

72. OT

BETWEEN THE RIVERS SECTION

NEAREST TOWNS: Van Buren, Hurricane Creek (Carter, Ripley and Oregon Counties).

DIRECTIONS: The northern entry point is on Hwy 60 approximately 3.5 miles west of Van Buren. From that point, the trail leads southwest to Forest Service Road 3152 near Hurricane Creek. Trailhead parking is provided at Hwy 60 and at Sinking Creek Lookout Tower approximately one mile west of Hwy J. Limited roadside parking is also possible at the southern end of the trail on FR 3152.

TRAIL DESCRIPTION: This 30-mile section of the Ozark Trail connects to the Current River section to the north and to the Eleven Point River section to the south. Half of the section is in the Doniphan Ranger District of the U.S. Forest Service.

From Hwy 60, the trail route is south for the first 13 miles winding through tributaries of the Current River: Wildhorse Hollow, Chilton Creek, Devil's Run and Big Barren Creek. The trail then heads west along the north prong of Cedar Bluff Creek. The trail gently climbs out of Cedar Bluff drainage and crosses a major ridge that divides the Current River watershed and the Eleven Point River watershed. The last 8.5 miles proceed southwest along Gold Mine Hollow, the ridge above Kelly Hollow, and Fox Hollow before ending on FR 3152 above Hurricane Creek.

HIGHLIGHTS: Just five miles south of here is Big Spring. This is the largest single-outlet spring in the United States. Sinking Creek Lookout Tower is at the trailhead and parking area.

HAZARDS: Watch for fallen trees.

AREA INFORMATION: Within Mark Twain National Forest, Doniphan Ranger District. The nearest improved campsites are located at Big Spring, and at Watercress Spring Recreation Area.

ADDITIONAL THOUGHTS: Expect to see horses on this trail.

CONTACT INFO: Doniphan Ranger District: (573) 592-1400.

DISTANCE: Approximately 30 miles long.

TERRAIN: This section of trail covers typical Ozark terrain: rock, gravel or hard pack sections with potentially exposed roots, hard turns and moderate to very technical sections.

RIDING TIME: You can take out at various access points. The first one is 6.5 miles out, the second is 13 miles out.

LAND STATUS: MTNF Doniphan/Eleven Point Ranger District.

SERVICES & ACTIVITIES: Close by Doniphan District facilities include Buffalo Creek Campground with three campsites, Float Camp (4.5 miles north of Doniphan on Hwy Y) and Deer Leap (5 miles north of Doniphan on Hwy Y) on the Current River with 29 campsites and swimming, fishing and floating, reserved pavilion and a boat launch at Deer Leap. Fourche Lake Campground is on a 49-acre lake. Ripley Lake Picnic Area has 20 picnic sites, 20-acre lake, drinking water and a boat ramp but no camping. Water Cress has 14 single units and three double units on Current River in Van Buren off Hwy 60. Facilities include drinking water, restrooms, fire rings, boat landing and swimming beach. There is a $7/single and $14/double camping fee (year-round facility).

Nearest improved campsites are at Big Spring (National Park Service), Watercress Spring Recreation Area, Greer Crossing Recreation Area, and McCormack Lake Recreation Area managed by the MTNF Doniphan/Eleven Point River Ranger District.

TRAILHEAD: At Van Buren. Go 3.5 miles west on Hwy 60 to the parking area.

RATING: Moderate.

MAPS: Request DNR brochure "OT - Between the Rivers Section."

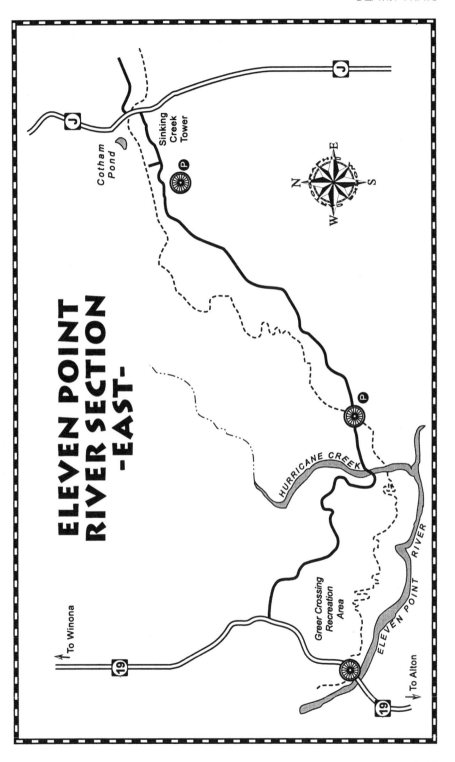

ELEVEN POINT
RIVER SECTION
-EAST-

Sinking
Creek
Tower

Cotham
Pond

HURRICANE CREEK

ELEVEN POINT RIVER

Greer Crossing
Recreation
Area

To Winona

To Alton

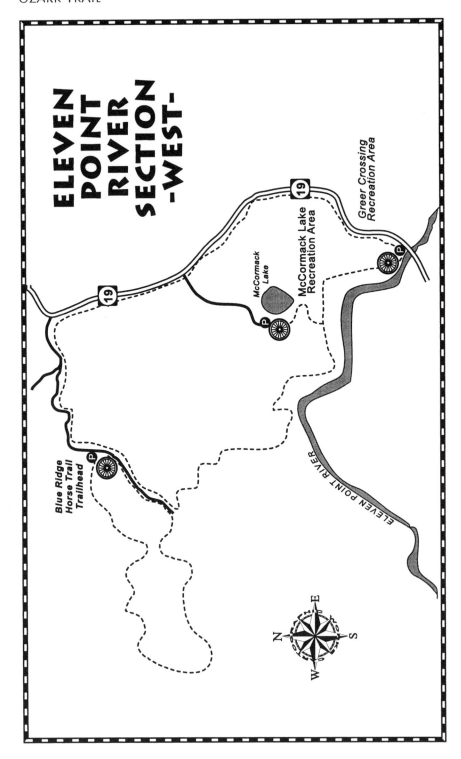

ELEVEN POINT RIVER SECTION -WEST-

McCormack Lake

McCormack Lake Recreation Area

Greer Crossing Recreation Area

Blue Ridge Horse Trail Trailhead

ELEVEN POINT RIVER

73. OT

ELEVEN POINT RIVER SECTION

NEAREST TOWNS: Greer and Alton (Oregon County).

DIRECTIONS: To get to the northern trailhead, take Hwy 19 to FR 3152 (approximately 6 miles east) of Hwy 19. To get to the southern trailhead, from Hwy 99, go 1 mile east on FR 3173, then 1 mile north on FR 4155.

Trailhead parking at FR 3152, Greer Recreation Area on Hwy 19, at McCormack Lake Recreation Area west of Hwy 19, and at the western terminus of FR 4155.

TRAIL DESCRIPTION: This 30-mile section of the Ozark Trail was completed in 1988. It links the Between the Rivers section to the east, and the planned North Fork Lake to the west. The Missouri portion of the Ozark Trails System will end with this section in Ozark county near Hwy 101 and North Fork Lake, a 2,200-acre lake with 200 acres in Missouri and 2,000 acres in Arkansas. The trail will then continue south into Arkansas on the 165-mile-long Ozark Highlands Trail (OHT).

The trail proceeds south from Hurricane Creek and FR 3152 for 10 miles through rugged slopes and drainages leading into the Eleven Point National Scenic River. Greer Recreation Area is located at mile 10. Proceed south to bluff view at mile 12 with a one-mile spur to McCormack Lake. The trai continues west along Eleven Point River passing Bockman Spring at mile 20, which is part of the Spring Creek drainage, which comprises the last 10 miles of this section. The trail ends near state Hwy 99 on FR 4155.

HIGHLIGHTS: This is a gorgeous stretch, with views of the Eleven Point and a crossing at Hurricane Creek.

HAZARDS: Keep your eyes open for high water, stinging nettle and snakes.

AREA INFORMATION: Hiking and equestrian use. Lakes, hiking trails, Eleven Point River recreational activities including boating, canoeing, swimming, floating and fishing.

ADDITIONAL THOUGHTS: This area is loaded with springs, both in wet and dry weather. This trail also passes Greer Springs, the second-largest spring in Missouri. Follow the sign and rough trail to check it out. Neaby, check out the 18.5-mile White's Creek Trail in the 16,500-acre Irish Wilderness (sorry, no mountain biking).

CONTACT INFO: Mark Twain National Forest, U.S. Park Service, Doniphan/Eleven Point River Ranger District Office, 1104 Walnut St., Doniphan, MO 63935. (573) 996-2153. Winona Office, Rte 1, Box 1908, Winona, MO 65588. (573) 325-4233.
DISTANCE: 30 miles long. It drops off in the middle of nowhere, with 2-3 miles to get to the next service road.
TERRAIN: Along ridges and hills.
RIDING TIME: A few hours to all day.
LAND STATUS: Mark Twain National Forest Doniphan/Eleven Point River Ranger District.
SERVICES & ACTIVITIES: Eleven Point River boat launches at Thomasville, Cane Bluff, Boomhole, Greer Crossing, Turners Mill (N and S), McDowell, Whitten, Riverton East and Hwy 142. Equestrian use on part of this section of the Ozark Trail and Blue Ridge Horse trail. Greer Campground is at the middle of the trail and there's a campground at McCormick Lake, too.
TRAILHEAD: At picnic area or at the boat launch at Greer.
RATING: Moderate.
MAPS: Request the DNR brochure "OT - Eleven Point River Section." Or contact the MTNF Winona office for topo maps: U.S. Forest Service, Eleven Point Ranger District, RR 1 Box 1908, Winona, MO 65588. (573) 325-4233.

74. OT

NORTH FORK RIVER SECTION

NEAREST TOWN: Pomona (Howell County).
DIRECTIONS: From Pomona, take Route P going west about 1 mile to the trailhead. Watch for signs.
TRAIL DESCRIPTION: Open except where it passes through wilderness areas. This trail is still being developed. Call the trail coordinator at DNR for more information before heading down to check out this trail. It hooks up with Ridge Runner Trail and Devil's Back Bone Wilderness Area, which does not allow MTBs.
HIGHLIGHTS: Pine forests, dry creek crossings and Lover's Leap overlook.
HAZARDS: Be cautious around bluffs and on slick rock.
ADDITIONAL THOUGHTS: North Fork Campground is nearby. About 15 miles from West Plains.
CONTACT INFO: Mark Twain National Forest Winona Ranger District: (417) 469-3155.
DISTANCE: 10 miles between Pomona and Route AP to Hammond Campground.
TERRAIN: Mostly gentle hills.
RIDING TIME: 2 hours.
LAND STATUS: Mark Twain National Forest.
SERVICES & ACTIVITIES: Gas station and mini-mart nearby. Willow Springs and West Plains have full services.
TRAILHEAD: Look for signs from Route P.
RATING: Easy to moderate.

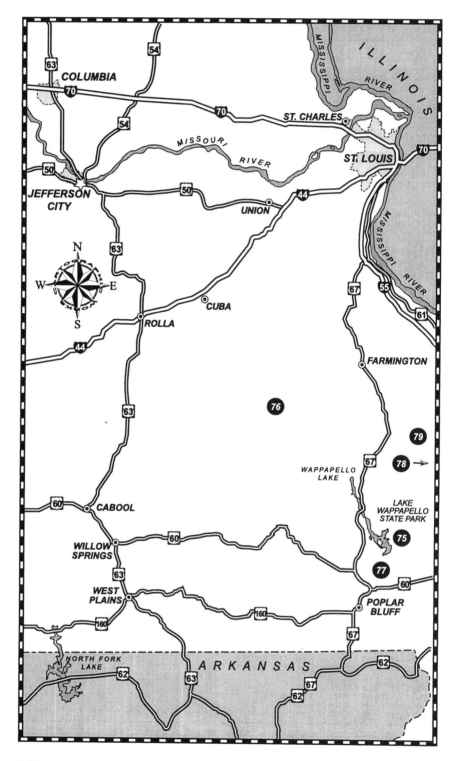

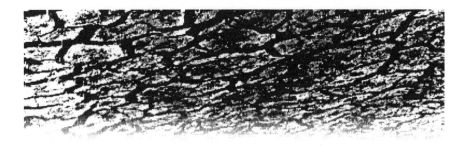

SOUTHEAST REGION TRAILS

75. LAKE WAPPAPELLO STATE PARK TRAIL

NEAREST TOWN: Poplar Bluff (Wayne County).
DIRECTIONS: Lake Wappapello State Park is located at the end of State Road 172 just off of Hwy 67 in southeast Missouri. To get there, go 16 miles north of Poplar Bluff on Hwy 67, and head 9 miles east on Hwy 172.
TRAIL DESCRIPTION: The trailhead for the 15-mile loop is on the right of the main park road at the bottom of a hill just before you pass the park office (if you're not careful, you'll miss it). Approximately half of the trail winds around the steep hills along the banks of Lake Wappapello, providing many excellent views of the lake. There are no climbs on the trail greater than 150 vertical feet or so, but some of the climbs can be quite steep. In all, the trail is almost entirely single track, is in very good shape and is a joy to ride. There is also a 5.5-mile (one-way) trail to the backpack camp, so you may be sharing the trail with a few backpackers.

Tucked at the southern end of the 8,600-acre Wappapello Lake, the park's scenic Ozark terrain gives hikers and backpackers hours of enjoyment, and the lake offers some of the best fishing in southeast Missouri. The 1,854-acre park has campsites, kitchen-equipped cabins and a marina with a complete stock of fishing supplies.

Several miles of hiking and backpacking trails wind through Lake Wappapello State Park. Lake Wappapello Trail, designed for hiking, backpacking, equestrian and all-terrain bicycling, wanders 15 miles through varied and rugged Ozark upland terrain. The Allison Cemetery Trail is a 3.5-mile hiking trail that follows the lake edge and goes past Allison Cemetery and up the ridge. The two-mile Asher Creek Trail incudes a hike along the waterfowl refuge area of the lake, and the half-mile Lake View Trail offers hikers a scenic, less strenuous route to follow.

HIGHLIGHTS: Mature forests and a great lake view. The cemetery is an interesting side trip and makes an excellent place to take a break (from five minutes to eternity).
HAZARDS: Flooding lake levels.
AREA INFORMATION: The area in and around Lake Wappapello State Park was originally settled by various North American Indian tribes, including the Shawnee, Cherokee, Osage

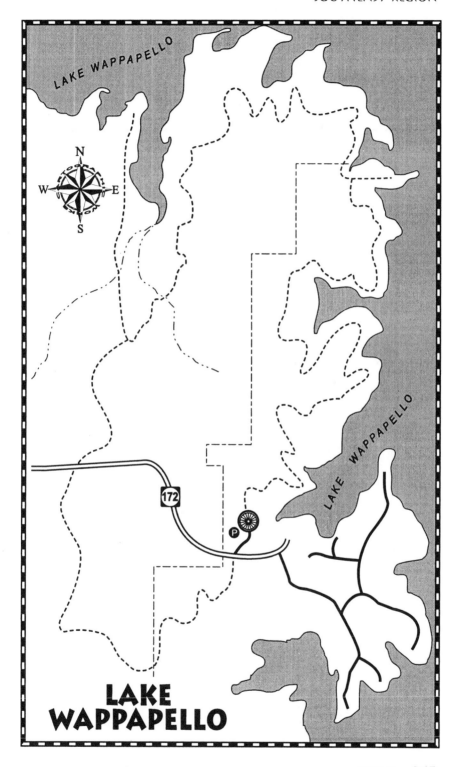

LAKE WAPPAPELLO

LAKE WAPPAPELLO

LAKE WAPPAPELLO

172

P

LAKE WAPPAPELLO

and Delaware. Throughout most of its early history, the region was used as hunting grounds, and legend has it that the town of Wappapello was named after a friendly Shawnee chief who hunted the forests during pioneer days.

The first pioneer, Isaac Kelly, came to the area in 1802, and in 1813 he received 640 acres from the U.S. government through recognition of occupancy. Settlers cut timber and farmed the land, and soon the Frisco Railroad established the town of Wappapello as a railway station. The nearby lake, constructed in the 1940s, was named for the town.

The state park itself comprises 1,854 acres of oak-hickory forest on the Allison Peninsula in the Wappapello Reservoir area. The land was owned by the Allison family from after the Civil War until the early 20th century. The state began leasing the property from the U.S. Army Corps of Engineers in 1957, and the area has been used as a nature area and a water recreation area ever since.

The valleys and chert hillsides of the upland forests contain tree varieties characteristic of the southern Ozark plain and the southeastern coastal plains. These include white, black, southern red and willow oaks; shagbark and pignut hickory; red buckeye, beech and tulip trees. Vegetation in the park comprises ferns, small yellow lady-slippers and other orchids in the shaded areas, bird's-foot violets, pussy's toes and Dutchman's breeches on the sunny slopes. Mistletoe, which grows in the black gum trees and sycamores along the edge of the lake, is a special feature rarely seen in Missouri.

An abundance of waterfowl may be seen along Asher Creek and in the nearby cove, which is designated as a winter waterfowl refuge. Visitors should watch for wintering birds, such as eagles, ospreys and a number of duck species, including mallards, buffleheads, ring-necked ducks, redheads and canvasbacks. Other inhabitants include great blue herons, multitudes of songbirds, and barred and great horned owls. A variety of wildlife lives in the park, including beaver, turkey, white-tailed deer and many small animals.

ADDITIONAL THOUGHTS: If you plan on biking Lake Wappapello in the spring or summer, make sure to bring plenty of bug repellent and soap and water to wash off with. The mosquitoes and posion ivy can be bad here.

CONTACT INFO: Lake Wappapello State Park, Williamsville, MO 63967. (573) 297-3232. Cabin reservations: (573) 297-3247.

DISTANCE: 15-mile loop.

TERRAIN: Some steep climbs and challenging descents. Lots of off-camber technical sections—don't fall in the lake!
RIDING TIME: 2 - 4 hours.
LAND STATUS: Department of Natural Resources.
SERVICES & ACTIVITIES: Two campgrounds—one perched on the ridge and one nestled near the lake—offer scenic views of the area. The park has tent and trailer campsites, some basic and some with electrical hookups; two campsites are designed for physically disabled visitors. Facilities in the campgrounds include two sanitary dumping stations, hot showers, modern restrooms, laundry facilities and a wood lot. Campsites are available on a first-come, first-served basis. Maximum continuous stay is limited to 15 days. A daily fee is charged and should be paid at the park office after the site has been selected.

Eight cabins are available for rent from April 1 to October 31. Each is air-conditioned and heated and is equipped with linens, kitchen supplies, picnic tables and grills. Seven of the cabins sleep six people, and one sleeps 10. Reservations are required and may be made by calling the concessionaire's office at (636) 297-3247 or the Department of Natural Resources at 1 (800) 334-6946.

The main peninsula of the park offers many ways to enjoy the lake. A fully equipped marina and store rents fishing boats, pontoons and motors and sells fishing tackle, food and other merchandise. A nearby 150-foot sand beach is ideal for swimming and a paved boat ramp is available for visitor use. Swimmers and boaters have easy access to the picnic area, which includes 25 picnic sites, a shelter and playground equipment.

TRAILHEAD: To the right of the main park road at the bottom of the hill. Be careful not to miss it!
RATING: Moderate.

76. MARK TWAIN NATIONAL FOREST

SUTTON BLUFF ATV TRAILS

NEAREST TOWN: Centerville (Reynolds County).
DIRECTIONS: Approximately 5 miles north of Centerville. To get there, head north on Hwy 21. Go 8 miles on FR 2233, turn left (south) on FR 2236, then go 3 miles to the campground. Follow the signs to the National Forest Campground and Sutton Bluff Campground. The Sutton Bluff Campground is the hub of the whole trail system.
TRAIL DESCRIPTION: This spread-out area has a trail system comprised of a series of 12 numbered trails. Once you reach the Sutton Bluff Campground, the trails are clearly marked and you will want to pick up a detailed map of the area from the park office of the campground.

This series of trails passes through general Ozark topography. Trails generally run from a ridge top into a drainage and then back out again. Some trails originally followed old logging roads, which have grown up and are now just a trail. Most go from ridge top into a bottom or contour down to the bottom. Some have switchbacks.

Some trail sections have been recently relocated, as the ranger district is trying to combat erosion problems from water runoff. The district is trying to relocate steep sections to an average of 10 percent or less grades.

In other words, there's short steep stretches, but the trail is primarily rolling hill topography. Keep in mind these trails were originally designed for ATVs and motorcycles, so some of the steep climbs and drops may seem a bit extreme on a mountain bike.

Trail 1 (Wolf Creek Trail), is a great place to start your day's ride. It is probably the most interesting trail, with short climbs, a lot of variety and a lot of tight turns. There's plenty of tight turns and twists and no straight sections. This is definitely a fun, technical trail and was not built for speed freaks. You will probably not average as many miles per hour as on, say, the Berryman. This is slow traveling, with a lot of side slope trail. Be sure and check out the Trail 4,5 & 6 complex as well.

HIGHLIGHTS: Several trails follow along streams and cross bridges. Very scenic areas and vistas. FR 2233 used to be considered a scenic drive—until the budget was cut back.

HAZARDS: Loose rocks, mud holes and motorized traffic. Watch for the water bars and dips that aid drainage.

AREA INFORMATION: This is a great campground and would serve as a great home base while you're riding all of the trails in this region.

ADDITIONAL THOUGHTS: Watch out for motorcycles. Most of these trails are fairly technical, so high-speed collisions are unlikely, but wear a helmet nonetheless.

CONTACT INFO: Mark Twain National Forest Salem District: (573) 729-6656.

DISTANCE: 12 trails range from 0.5 mile to 6 miles, for a total of 20 miles of trail. If you really explore, you'll probably find closer to 25 miles.

TERRAIN: Hardpacked dirt, loose gravel and some rocky sections.

RIDING TIME: All afternoon.

LAND STATUS: Mark Twain National Forest.

SERVICES & ACTIVITIES: Concession at campground. Maps available at concession stand, at ranger district offices and in Rolla.

TRAILHEAD: Sutton Bluff Campground.

RATING: Moderate.

77. UNIVERSITY FOREST CONSERVATION AREA

EQUESTRIAN TRAIL

NEAREST TOWN: Poplar Bluff (Butler & Wayne Counties).

DIRECTIONS: University Forest consists of five tracts. From Poplar Bluff, take Hwy 67 north for 13-15 miles. Go east on Hwy 172 for 4.5 miles. Go south on Route W for 3 miles to the parking area on the left. This horse trail system can also be reached from other parking areas throughout this 7,149-acre conservation area.

TRAIL DESCRIPTION: There are trails throughout the area, consisting of a large loop trail in its south half, south of Asher Creek. The north portion of this conservation area, near the Wappapello Lake Trail, consists of several trails that are not all connected. Although primarily an equestrian trail, cyclists may use the same trails always giving right-of-way to horses.

AREA INFORMATION: This area is located near the south side of Lake Wappapello and is approximately 10 miles north of Poplar Bluff. This 7,149-acre area was originally endowed to the University of Missouri by the federal government as part of the Agriculture College Act of 1862. The School of Forestry, Fisheries and Wildlife took responsibility for the area in the early 1900s and in 1946 began managing the area for research and as a forestry summer camp.

The Conservation Department acquired the area in 1988. The area is primarily covered with oak and hickory forest, with a scattering of shortleaf pines. Abundant deer, turkey, pileated woodpeckers and other typical Ozark wildlife will be found here.

ADDITIONAL THOUGHTS: Bicycles are permitted only on roads and trails open to vehicular traffic and horseback riding and on service roads posted closed to motorized vehicles, except when further restricted by posting.

CONTACT INFO: Department of Conservation Southeast Region Piedmont Office: (573) 856-4142.

DISTANCE: 21.5 miles.

RIDING TIME: 3 - 8 hours.

LAND STATUS: Missouri Department of Conservation.

SERVICES & ACTIVITIES: No restrooms, camping or water.

RATING: Moderate to difficult.

78. APPLE CREEK CONSERVATION AREA

EQUESTRIAN TRAIL

NEAREST TOWN: New Wells (Cape Girardeau County).

DIRECTIONS: Located in northeast Cape Girardeau County 3 miles east of New Wells on Route CC. North of Jackson, take I-55 Exit 105 to Hwy 61. Go north on Hwy 61 for 8 miles. Then go east on Route CC for 5 miles. Go south on County Road 525 for 1 mile. Turn left on the gravel road and park at the horse trail parking lot.

TRAIL DESCRIPTION: This 2,100-acre area is characterized by steep hills and narrow valleys, with about 2.5 miles of Apple Creek forming the conservation area's northern border. This trail consists of old service and logging roads. Efforts are made to keep the trails mowed. It passes from upland oak-hickory forests to bottomland forests, with several scenic stretches passing through openings, valley fields and past corn, wheat and bean fields. The only water crossing is the occasional wet-weather spring. This is primarily a horse trail, so always give right-of-way to them.

HIGHLIGHTS: Breaking out of the forest into a wide valley field.

AREA INFORMATION: The Conservation Department has created ponds and planted food plots within the forest to provide additional food sources for wildlife. Boundaries are marked from tree to tree with blue paint or signs.

Nearby Apple Creek drains into the Mississippi River. The boat ramp and fishing access are popular spots for catching white bass.

ADDITIONAL THOUGHTS: Bring plenty of water and a repair kit. Bicycles are permitted only on roads and trails open to vehicular traffic and horseback riding and on service roads posted closed to motorized vehicles, except when further restricted by posting.

CONTACT INFO: Missouri Department of Conservation Southeast Region Perryville Office: (573) 547-4537.

DISTANCE: 5-mile horse trail.

TERRAIN: Steep hills and narrow valleys.

RIDING TIME: 2-hour ride to all afternoon.

LAND STATUS: Missouri Department of Conservation.

SERVICES & ACTIVITIES: Primitive camping. No restrooms.

TRAILHEAD: Look for the horse trail parking lot.

RATING: Moderate.

79. CASTOR RIVER CONSERVATION AREA

EQUESTRIAN TRAIL

NEAREST TOWN: Marble Hill (Bollinger County).

DIRECTIONS: To get to the main tract from Fredericktown, take Hwy 67 south for 30 miles. Go east on Hwy 34 for 16 miles, then go south on Route Y until the pavement ends. Continue for 0.5 mile on this gravel road to the horse trail parking lot. Or, from Marble Hill take Hwy 34 west and follow the signs.

TRAIL DESCRIPTION: Castor River Horse Trail is at the southern end of this conservation area, which is comprised of eight separate land parcels totaling 9,123 acres, southwest of Marble Hill. This is an upland oak and hickory forest. The Castor River runs nearby, but not through the area. Cyclists may use the same trails as equestrians always giving right-of-way to horses.

HIGHLIGHTS: Visit Blue Pond Natural Area—the deepest, natural sinkhole in Missouri, which is filled with clear blue water. Some theorists contend it was formed by the New Madrid Earthquake. MTB'ers aren't allowed to ride within this natural area, so walk them in. There is also a 1.5-acre fen and numerous dry sink holes here.

HAZARDS: Wear hunter's orange during hunting season. This is a popular spot for deer and turkey hunting.

AREA INFORMATION: Ride the trail so that you start out heading east, so that you can visit Double Sink approximately 2 miles into your ride. Heading west will take you on 12 miles of the loop trail before you get to the Double Sink.

ADDITIONAL THOUGHTS: Bicycles permitted only on roads and trails open to vehicular traffic and horseback riding and on service roads posted closed to motorized vehicles, except when further restricted by posting.

CONTACT INFO: MDOC Cape Girardeau Office: (573) 290-5730.

DISTANCE: 15-mile loop trail.

TERRAIN: Steep, broken hills and stony soil.

RIDING TIME: All afternoon.

LAND STATUS: Missouri Department of Conservation.

SERVICES & ACTIVITIES: Primitive camping. No restrooms.

TRAILHEAD: Follow signs to horse trail parking.

RATING: Moderate.

NEW TRAILS JUST IN!

I've realized that, in-deed, a book is never done. Here are three more trails to check out. I will update this book, so if you find a great new ride, better directions or additional stretches of trail, please write me care of: Pebble Publishing, P.O. Box 2, Rocheport, MO 65279. (573) 698-3903. Fax: (573) 698-3108. I'll send you a bunch of free goodies.

80. CAVE HOLLOW & 81. PIRTLE SPRINGS

NEAREST TOWN: Warrensburg (Johnson County).
DIRECTIONS: Both rides are within Warrensburg city limits. If you're a CMSU student, these are great local rides. To get there from I-70, take Hwy 13 south all the way to Warrensburg.
TRAIL DESCRIPTION: Both are hardpacked single track. Cave Hollow is a more established city park, with trails in the back. Pirtle Springs is a CMSU-owned forest where local riders have been bushwacking trails, so it's not a maintained trail.
CONTACT INFO: Call Warrensburg Parks and Rec at (660) 747-7178 or the city at (660) 747-9136. Call CMSU's operator at (660) 543-4111 for directions to Pirtle Springs.
DISTANCE: 2 miles of moderate, looping, interconnecting trail.

82. ARROWHEAD MTB PARK
NEAREST TOWN: Kansas City (Jackson County).
DIRECTIONS: This area is across the railroad tracks from the Truman Sports Complex. It is right off of I-70 between I-435 and Blueridge Cutoff. If you are on I-70, take 1-435 south to Raytown Road. Exit onto Raytown Road going east. Watch for the park on the north side of the street.
TRAIL DESCRIPTION: A 20-mile + loop trail. Constantly being expanded. Contact the Jackson County Parks and Rec for more information. (816) 795-8200 or email stalwil@gw.co.jackson.mo.us.

━━ MISSOURI BIKE CLUBS ━━

Consult this list, scan local bike shop bulletin boards, ask bike shop folks and check your local phone book for more bike club information.

Blue River Bicycle Club
Ariel Mendez
12311 State Line Road
Kansas City, MO 64145
(816) 942-4442

Capitol City Cycling Club
Sandy Wulff • P.O. Box 1202
Holts Summit, MO 65043
(573) 896-5222

Clayton Cycling Club
 /Mesa Cycles • 7811 Clayton Rd
Saint Louis, MO 63117
(314) 645-4447

Columbia Bicycle Club
Max Earl • P.O. Box 110
Columbia, MO 65205
(573) 446-3056

Dirt Gypsies/Women's Riding Network
1901 Ridge Lane
Pacific, MO 63069
(314) 707-4422

Earth Riders
Andrew C. Stokes
7405 N Woodland Ave
Gladstone, MO 64118
(816) 231-0996
E-mail: acstokes@qni.com

Folks on Spokes
734 Strafford Ridge Drive
Manchester, MO 63021
(636) 861-0558

Hostelling International/AYH
7187 Manchester Road
St. Louis, MO 63143
(314) 644-4660

Kansas City Bicycle Club
Lou Burkhart
(816) 436-5606

Kirksville Bicycle Club
2410 N Oak Ln
Kirksville, MO 63501

Lasers Cycling Club
1226 Havenhurst Rd
Manchester, MO 63011

McDonnel D. Bicycle Club
2901 Olde Gloucester Dr
St. Charles, MO 63301

Missouri Bicycle Federation
Karen Giarratano • P.O. Box 104871
Jefferson City, MO 65110
(573) 636-4488

Missouri Fat Tire Series
Heather Atkinson • 5126 NE Antioch
Kansas City, MO 64119
(816) 455-2453

Mo Bicycle Racing Association
15403 Clover Ridge Dr
Chesterfield, MO 63017

Ozark Cycling Club (Road Bike Only)
2246 S. Kansas
Springfield, MO 65807
(417) 886-0080

Ozark Cyclist Racing (MTB Only)
2101 W. Chesterfield Blvd A-102
Springfield, MO 65807

Rolla Bicycle Assoc.
40 Hawthorne Rd
Rolla, MO 65401

224 — SHOW ME MOUNTAIN BIKING

Springbike Bicycle Club
John Davis • 1134 S Cedarbrook Ave
Springfield, MO 65804
(417) 882-9568

St. Louis BicycleWORKS
4100 Shenandoah • St. Louis, MO
E-mail: stlbwork@fastrans.net

St. Louis Cycling Club
12132 Wesmeade Dr
Maryland Heights, MO 63043
(314) 739-5180

TC (Touring Cyclist) Tours
11816 St. Charles Rock Road
Bridgeton, MO 63044
(314) 739-5180

Trail Advocacy • 2 S Grim Ct
Kirksville, MO 63501

UMR Bike Club • 202 University
Rolla, MO 65401 • (573) 341-4209

NATIONAL BIKE CLUBS

Adventure Cycling Association
Gary MacFadden, Director
P.O. Box 8308 • Missoula, MT 59807
(406) 721-1776

Bicycle Federation of America
1818 R St. NW
Washington, DC 20009
(202) 332-6986

Bicycle Helmet Safety Institute (BHSI)
Randy Swart, Director
4611 Seventh Street South
Arlington, VA 22204
(703) 486-0100

Bicycle Industry Organization
1526 Spruce St. Second Floor
Boulder, CO 80302
(303) 444-4246

International Christian Cycling Club
Marlen Wells, President
3739 E 4th Ave.
Denver, CO 80206
(303) 321-1014

International Mountain Bicycling
Association (IMBA)
P.O. Box 7578
Boulder, CO 80306
(303) 545-9011

League of American Bicyclists
190 W Ostend St. Ste 120
Baltimore, MD 21230
(410) 539-3399

National Collegiate Cycling Assoc.
Matt Donadio
146 Beaver Hall
University Park, PA 16802
(814) 862-6116

National Cycle League International
532 Laguardia Place, Suite 162
New York, NY 10012
(212) 777-3611

National Off-Road Bicycle Assoc. (NORBA)
One Olympic Plaza
1750 E Boulder St.
Colorado Springs, CO 80909
(719) 578-4717

Tandem Club of America (TCA)
Jack & Susan Goertz, Editors
2220 Vanessa Drive
Birmingham, AL 35242
(205) 991-7766

United States Olympic Committee
1750 E Boulder St.
Colorado Springs, CO 80909

━━ MISSOURI BIKE SHOPS ━━
Listed Alphabetically by Region

ST. LOUIS & EASTERN REGION

A & M Cyclery
4282 Arsenal St
Saint Louis, MO 63116
(314) 776-1144

A-1 Bicycle Sales
10211 Manchester Rd
Saint Louis, MO 63122
(314) 821-0216

Alpine Shop
601 East Lockwood
Webster Groves, MO 63119
(314) 962-7229

Baden Bicycle Center
8204 N Broadway
Saint Louis, MO 63147
(314) 383-3886

Ballwin Schwinn & Trek
15216 Manchester Rd
Ballwin, MO 63011
(314) 391-2666

Bicycle Basics
2107 Hwy K
O Fallon, MO 63366
(314) 240-9579

Bicycles of Kirkwood
207 N Kirkwood Rd
Kirkwood, MO 63122
(314) 821-3460

Big Bend Bicycle
8748 Big Bend Blvd
Saint Louis, MO 63119
(314) 961-7331

Big Shark Bicycle Company
6681 Delmar Blvd
Saint Louis, MO 63130
(314) 862-1188

Bike & Fitness Center - Des Peres
12011 Manchester Rd
Saint Louis, MO 63131
(314) 965-1444

Bike & Fitness Center - U City-Clayton
8200 Delmar Blvd
Saint Louis, MO 63124
(314) 727-8458

Bike & Fitness Center - Ellisville
355 Ozark Trails
Manchester, MO 63011
(314) 227-7266

Bike & Fitness Center - St. Peters
3819 Mexico Rd
Saint Peters, MO 63376
(314) 928-1127

Bikes Unlimited
4023 Jeffco Blvd
Arnold, MO 63010
(314) 464-2453

Bridgeton Cyclery
12011 Saint Charles Rock Rd
Bridgeton, MO 63044
(314) 739-3030

Crystal City Cyclery
2292 N Truman Blvd
Crystal City, MO 63019
(314) 937-6201

Cyclists Garage
706 Montbrook Court
O'Fallon, MO 63366
(314) 281-9543

Granada Cyclery & Fitness
62 Four Seasons Shopping Center
Chesterfield, MO 63017
(314) 434-9911

Granada Cyclery & Fitness
3139 W Clay
Saint Charles, MO 63301
(636) 946-7442

Johns Bike Shop
Box 152 C
Ewing, MO 63440
(573) 494-3636

Katy Bike Rental Inc
2998 S Highway 94
Defiance, MO 63341
(636) 987-2673

Maplewood Bicycle Sales & Service
7534 Manchester Rd
Saint Louis, MO 63143
(314) 781-9566

Mesa Cycles
1035 South Big Bend
Saint Louis, MO 63117
(314) 645-4447

Momentum Cycles
384 Mid Rivers Mall Drive
Saint Peters, MO 63376
(636) 397-7433

Revolution Cycles
2033 Hiawatha Ave
Saint Louis, MO 63143

Scenic Cycles
203 Depot St
Marthasville, MO 63357
(636) 433-2909

South County Cyclery Inc
9985 Lin Ferry Rd
Saint Louis, MO 63123
(314) 843-5586

South Side Cyclery
6969 Gravois Ave
Saint Louis, MO 63116
(314) 481-1120

Sun & Ski Sports
12380 Olive Street Rd
Saint Louis, MO 63141
(314) 434-9044

Touring Cyclist - Augusta
5533 Water Street
Augusta, MO
(636) 228-4882

Touring Cyclist - Bridgeton
11816 Saint Charles Rock Rd
Bridgeton, MO 63044
(314) 739-5183

Touring Cyclist - Florissant
11701 W Florissant Ave
Florissant, MO 63033
(314) 921-1717

Touring Cyclist - Manchester
14367 Manchester Rd
Ballwin, MO
(636) 394-6477

Touring Cyclist - Richmond Heights
1107 S Big Bend Blvd
Saint Louis, MO
(314) 781-7973

Touring Cyclist - South County
5809 S Lindbergh Blvd
Saint Louis, MO
(314) 894-4844

Touring Cyclist - St Charles
104 S Main St
Saint Charles, MO
(636) 949-9630

Webster Outdoor Gear
111 W Lockwood Ave
Webster Groves, MO 63119
(314) 961-4742

Wheels West
16019 Manchester Rd
Ballwin, MO 63011
(636) 391-8530

COLUMBIA &
CENTRAL REGION

Cycle Extreme Inc
19 S. Sixth Street
Columbia, MO 65201
(573) 874-7044

Golden Rocket Bicycle Shop
113 S Center St
Shelbina, MO 63468
(573) 588-4006

Hartsburg Cycle Depot
30 S. Second Street
Hartsburg, MO 65039
(573) 657-9599

J & D Bicycle Shop
610 Jefferson St
Jefferson City, MO 65101
(573) 635-4091

Jim's Bike & Key Shop
1002 N Old Hwy 63
Columbia, MO 65202 • (573) 442-7011

Trailside Café and Bike Rental
First and Pike
Rocheport, MO 65279
(573) 698-2702

Tryathletics
1605 Chapel Hill Road
Columbia, MO 65203
(573) 447-2453

Walt's Bicycle & Fitness
1217 Rogers St.
Columbia, MO 65201
(573) 886-9258

Young Bike Shop
214 N Franklin St
Kirksville, MO 63501
(660) 665-6412

KANSAS CITY &
WESTERN REGION

Bicycle Adventure
6222 N Chatham Ave
Kansas City, MO 64151
(816) 741-2400

Bicycle Haven
1215 W Elm St
Independence, MO 64050
(816) 461-7433

Bicycle Warehouse
11419 Strang Line Rd
Kansas City, MO 66215

Bike America
32 SE Third Street
Lee's Summit, MO 64063

Bike Stop Bicycle Stores
Blue Springs
925 SW US Highway 40
Blue Springs, MO 64015
(816) 224-8588

Bike Werks • 543 E 5th St
Sedalia, MO 65301
(816) 827-0500

Bikesource
11912 West 119th Street
Overland Park, KS 66213
(913) 451-1515

Bikesource • 231 SE Main
Lee's Summit, MO 64063
(816) 525-6000

Biscari Brothers Bicycles - Liberty
884 S 291 Highway
Liberty, MO 64068
(816) 792-8877

Blood, Sweat & Gears
1110 S Odell Ave
Marshall, MO 65340

Bicycle Shack
10415 Blue Ridge Blvd
Kansas City, MO 64134
(816) 761-3233

Bicycles By Saverino
2402 Messanie St
Saint Joseph, MO 64501

Bike Shack
10415 Blue Ridge Blvd
Kansas City, MO 64134
(816) 761-3233

Bike Stop Bicycle Stores - KC Area
4013 Sterling Ave
Raytown, MO 64133
(816) 353-8448

Cecil's Cyclery
704 S Ohio Ave
Sedalia, MO 65301
(816) 826-3987

Crank & Pedal
110 E Torrance St
Maryville, MO
(660) 582-8323

Leawood Bicycles
12311 State Line Rd
Kansas City, MO 64145
(816) 942-4442

Midwest Cyclery Inc
3957 Broadway St
Kansas City, MO 64111
(816) 931-4653

Pace Bicycle Haven
1215 W Lexington-Elm Ave
Independence, MO 64050
(816) 461-7433

Peddlers Bike Shop
139 E Lexington Ave
Independence, MO 64050
(816) 254-6855

Prairie Pedalers
9708 E 77th St
Raytown, MO 64138

Ride Bicycles
2320 N Belt Hwy
Saint Joseph, MO 64506
(816) 233-1718

River Market Cyclery
315 East Third Street
Kansas City, MO 64106
(816) 842-2453

Sunshine Bicycle Of Liberty
352 S 291 Highway
Liberty, MO 64068
(816) 792-1331

The Wheel Cyclery
5126 NE Antioch Rd
Kansas City, MO 64119
(816) 455-2453

SPRINGFIELD & OZARK MOUNTAINS REGION

A & B Cycle Inc
3201 S Campbell Ave
Springfield, MO 65807
(417) 881-5940

A & B Cycle Inc
220 West Walnut
Springfield, MO 65806
(417) 866-6621

Bicycle Specialists
308 Hogdon Rd
Joplin, MO 64801
(417) 781-1664

Cycles Unlimited
1254 East Republic Road
Springfield, MO 65804
(417) 887-3560

Jennings Bicycle Shop
1249 S Garrison Ave
Carthage, MO 64836
(417) 358-4269

Joplin Bike & Fitness
2629 S Main St • Joplin, MO

Ozark Cyclist
2101 W. Chesterfield Blvd. Suite A102
Springfield, MO 65807
(417) 886-0080

Sunshine Cycle Bike Shop
1926 E Sunshine St
Springfield, MO 65804
(417) 883-1113

Willard Bicycle Shop • 106 E Jackson
Willard, MO 65781 • (417) 742-4465

**ROLLA & OZARK
HIGHLANDS REGION**

Ozark Bicycles • 3926 Hwy 54
Across from KFC, near Jct. 54 & 42
Osage Beach, MO 65065
(573) 348-6221

World of Wheels • Rt. 1 Box 209B
Versailles, MO 65084 • (573) 378-6204

**OZARK TRAIL &
SOUTHEAST REGION**

Cape Bicycle Cycling and Fitness
2410 William St
Cape Girardeau, MO 63703
(573) 335-2453

Country Cycles • 1139 Vine St
Poplar Bluff, MO 63901
(573) 785-7400

Freshour Cycle Co.
949 River Birch Mall
Sikeston, MO 63801
(573) 471-3543

R & M Bicycle Shop
600 First St
Kennett, MO 63857
(573) 888-5914

Velo Girardeau
344 N Ellis St
Cape Girardeau, MO 63701

MISSOURI FAT TIRE SERIES

For information on the Missouri Fat Tire State Championship series, contact Heather Atkinson at (816) 455-2453, or write her at: Missouri Fat Tire State Championship, 5126 NE Antioch, KC, MO 64119.

NORBA STATE CHAMPIONSHIP SERIES

For information on the NORBA State Championship series, contact Steve Pittman at (314) 739-5180, or write him at: NORBA State Championship Series, Touring Cyclist, 11816 St. Charles Rock Road, Bridgeton, MO 63044.

— ADDITIONAL RESOURCES —

For free brochures and information on many aspects of Missouri nature, write the Missouri Department of Conservation at P.O. Box 180, Jefferson City, MO 65102. These brochures are a great way to learn about every species out there. They also have a free map called Outdoor Missouri, which highlights conservation areas, state parks, fishing accesses and national forests.

Conservation Federation of Missouri
728 W. Main
Jefferson City, MO 65101
(573) 634-2322

Department of Natural Resources
Division of State Parks
P.O. Box 176
Jefferson City, MO 65102
(573) 751-2479 or 1 (800) 334-6946
or 1 (800) 379-2419 (with TDD)

Division of Tourism
P.O. Box 1055
Jefferson City, MO 65102
(573) 751-4133. For trip planning,
call 1 (800) 877-1234

Katy Central Association
P.O. Box 872
Columbia, MO 65205
1 (888) 441-2023

Mark Twain National Forest
Forest Supervisor
401 Fairgrounds Road
Rolla, MO 65401
(573) 364-4621

Meramec River Recreation Association
41 South Central, Seventh Floor
Clayton, MO 63105
(314) 889-2874

Missouri Department of Conservation
P.O. Box 180
Jefferson City, MO 65102-0180
(573) 751-4115

Missouri Streams and Trails Association
Bill Oliver, Executive Director
P.O. Box 1478
Ballwin, MO 63022
(314) 458-1995 • Fax: (314) 225-2744

Ozark Greenways
Terry Whaley, Executive Director
P.O. Box 50733
Springfield, MO 65805
(417) 864-2014

Ozark National Scenic Riverways
Superintendent - National Park Service
P.O. Box 490
Van Buren, MO 63965
(573) 323-4236

Ozark Trails Council
Debbie Schnack
Planner and Trail Coordinator
Department of Natural Resources
Div. of State Parks • P.O. Box 176
Jefferson City, MO 65102
(573) 526-5743 • Fax: (573) 751-8656

Pebble Publishing, Inc.
P.O. Box 2
Rocheport, MO 65279
(573) 698-3903

U.S. Army Corps of Engineers
Rt 2 Box A
Wappapello, MO 63966-9603
(314) 222-8234

WEBSITES FOR RAINY DAY ARMCHAIR ODYSSEYS

Department of Natural Resources: www.state.mo.us/dnr/dsp/
homedesp.htm
Earthriders Mountain Bike Club Web Site. Kansas City based:
www.earthriders.org
Hostelling International/AYH: www.gatewayhiayh.org/
Interactive Katy Trail: www.katytrail.showmestate.com
Missouri Conservation Department Website:
www.conservation.state.mo.us
Missouri online: showmestate.com
Missouri Outdoor Magazine: www.thenerve2.com/outdoors
More state park information: www.mobot.org/stateparks/
This site includes descriptions and good maps for every state
park and historic site in Missouri.
More mountain bike info: ww.mtbinfo.com/trails/MO
St. Louis BicycleWORKS: www.home.fastrans.net/~stlbwork
The Nature Conservancy (Official): www.tnc.org/
Ozark Cycling Club: OzarkCyclist.com
Ozark Trail Site:
home.stlnet.com/~slluez/OTS.MOARK_main.html
Outside Magazine Online: www.outside.starwave.com/
Outdoor Activities in the St. Louis Area:
www.st-louis.mo.us/st-louis/outdoors.html
Order Midwest guidebooks online: Trailsidebooks.com
Quick access to MTNF campground information:
www.gorp.com/dow/eastern/mtw.htm

MISSOURI'S KATY TRAIL ACCESSIBLE FROM CYBERSPACE

Parts of the *Katy Trail Guidebook* are now available in a convenient online edition, called the *Interactive Katy Trail*, opening up the trail to 10 million "cyberhikers" worldwide, who surf the Internet for fun and information.

The site was developed by Global Image, Inc., an award-winning producer of sites on the Internet's World Wide Web, and Pebble Publishing.

The online guide, the first and most complete online rails-to-trails to hit the Internet, includes updates on trail conditions, area day trips and lots of gorgeous color photographs. There are also forums where people can meet, ask questions and talk about things like hiking, biking and where to find a place to stay.

Thousands of visitors have surfed by the site since its launch in December 1995. The site's designer, Alan Westenbroek, said, "We've received e-mail from people around the world who are planning trips to Missouri to check out the trail. Groups from other states have visited, who want to use the trail as a model for their own Rails-to-Trails projects."

Since the *Interactive Katy Trail* was launched, its innovative, content-packed design has garnered numerous awards including mentions in *USA Today,* Point Communications' Top 5 Percent of the Web award, Editor's Choice in Reader's Digest, an award from Gateway Trailnet in St. Louis and was ranked as one of PC Computing's Top 1,001 Sites. Dufur says he attributes the number of awards to the site's graphics, easy navigation and striking photography.

For people thinking about a vacation or adventure in Missouri this spring, the *Interactive Katy Trail* is a perfect starting point. The *Interactive Katy Trail* is accessible on the Internet's World Wide Web at: *www.katytrail.showmestate.com.*

BIBLIOGRAPHY

Cycle St. Louis newspaper. Various dates. Steve Pittman, editor. Published by Touring Cyclist. Free publication.

Guide to Cycling Kansas City, by Steve Katz, 1995, Cycle Write Enterprises. (Now distributed by Pebble Publishing, Inc.)

Guide to Cycling St. Louis, by Steve Katz, 1994, Cycle Write Enterprises. (Now distributed by Pebble Publishing, Inc.)

Missouri Department of Conservation website and various publications.

Missouri Department of Natural Resources website and various publications.

The Complete Katy Trail Guidebook, Fourth Edition, by Brett Dufur, 1998, Pebble Publishing, Inc.

The Fathead's Guide to Mountain Biking Missouri, by Gary Barnett and Brian Mais, 1995. Buffalo Mountain Publishing (no longer available).

The Mountain Biker's Guide to the Ozarks, by Steve Henry, 1993, Menasha Ridge Press and Falcon Press. (Part of Dennis Coello's America by Mountain Bike Series).

NOTES:

ABOUT THE AUTHOR

Brett Dufur is the author of *The Complete Katy Trail Guidebook,* now in its fourth edition, *Best of Missouri Hands,* and *Exploring Missouri Wine Country.* He is also co-author of *Daytrip Columbia, Daytrip St. Louis, River Valley Companion—A Nature Guide* and *Forgotten Missourians Who Made History.*

He is currently working on a book entitled *The River Revisited,* documenting the 1996 Lewis and Clark keelboat reenactment and comparing the Missouri River in 1804 to the present.

In addition to writing books, he is the editor and publisher at Pebble Publishing, a publishing house of regional interest books based in Rocheport, Missouri. He is also the editor-in-chief of the *Missouri Wine Country Journal* magazine. He has worked at *Costa Rica Guide* magazine, *Missouri Magazine, River Valley Review* and at several newspapers in Arkansas and Missouri, as well as *Constructor de Caminos*, a Latin American trade magazine.

Brett was born in Kansas City, Missouri. He received both his journalism degree and a degree in Latin American Studies from the University of Missouri–Columbia. He spends his off-hours getting tangled up in words, traveling and exploring with his girlfriend Tawnee, his dog Daisy and Matisse the 'rat in a cat suit.'

REDUCE, REUSE, RECYCLE

In creating this book, many steps were taken to reduce paper waste. Computers now make "paperless" offices a semi-reality. Paper scrap and early drafts of this book were recycled, and the paper stock for this book is 20 percent pre-consumer waste.

ABOUT THE PHOTOGRAPHER

Margo Carroll has been a photographer for as long as she can remember. She says what drives her is the en joyment she gets sharing what she sees with others.

Margo has raced bikes since she was 14, including BMX, road and mountain bikes—and has been ranked number 2 nationally.

"I enjoy mostly just riding, enjoying the sights, sounds and smells of the forest. Mountain biking is such a wonderful experience, it can take you places you will never see in a car. I enjoy riding in all the different seasons and enjoying the wildflowers or the quiet crispness of a winter day," Margo said.

Margo was also one of the founders of the Midwest Mountain Bike Club, back in the 1980's. This group was the first of its kind in this area and was instrumental in establishing mountain biking relationships with area land managers, and bringing people together. The Club also promoted a 12-race series each year and the State Championships for several years.

Today, Margo works with the Womens' Riding Network, a group of women who cycle in the St. Louis area. She is also a sales representative at Riteway Products, a division of GT. She has also recently completed a thorough expansion and revision of Steve Katz' Guide to Cycling St. Louis. Her updated book will be published by Pebble Publishing, Inc. during the summer of 1999.

Throughout her work and play, her goal remains the same. "I enjoy sharing the great joys of cycling with others. As Ghandi said, "We must be the change we wish to see in the world.' "

THE SHOW ME MISSOURI SERIES

A TO Z MISSOURI
—A dictionary-style look at Missouri place name origins

Abo to Zwanzig! Includes history for each town, pronunciations, population, county, post office dates and more. 220 pages. By Margot Ford McMillen. $14.95. ISBN: 0-9646625-4-X

THE COMPLETE KATY TRAIL GUIDEBOOK
—America's Longest Rail-to-Trail Project

The definitive guide to services, towns, people, places and history along Missouri's 200-mile Katy Trail. This completely revised and updated fourth edition covers the cross-state hiking and biking trail from Clinton to St. Charles. Includes maps, 80 photos and more. 192 pages. By Brett Dufur. $14.95. ISBN: 0-9646625-0-7

DAYTRIP COLUMBIA

Guide to hidden highlights, galleries, museums, towns, people and history in Columbia, Rocheport, Centralia and Boone County. Full of fun daytrips and inexpensive outings. Most trips are free or under $10. Includes maps and photos. 168 pages. By Pamela Watson. $12.95. ISBN: 0-9646625-2-3

DAYTRIP ILLINOIS—The tour guide standard for Illinois

Covers daytrips around the state, including annual events, travel tips, 60 photos and 20 maps. Daytrips to help you enjoy the best of the Land of Lincoln. Exhaustively researched. 420 pages. By Lee N. Godley and Patricia Murphy O'Rourke. $16.95. ISBN: 0-9651340-0-6

DAYTRIP MISSOURI—The tour guide standard for Missouri

Covers daytrips around the state, including annual events, travel tips, 60 photos and 20 maps. 224 pages. By Lee N. Godley and Patricia Murphy O'Rourke. $14.95. ISBN: 0-9651340-0-8

DAYTRIP ST. LOUIS

The new, definitive guide to "The Gateway of the West," including both downtown daytrips and highlights of those within 2 hours, including wine country, Illinois' Great River Road and more. 224 pages. By Brett Dufur. $14.95. ISBN: 1-891708-00-7

EXPLORING MISSOURI WINE COUNTRY

This guidebook to Missouri wine country profiles wineries, including how to get there, their histories, wine tips, home-brew recipes, dictionary of wine terms and more. Also lists nearby bed & breakfasts, services and state parks. 208 pages. By Brett Dufur. $14.95. ISBN: 0-9646625-6-6

THE SHOW ME MISSOURI SERIES

FORGOTTEN MISSOURIANS WHO MADE HISTORY

A book of short stories and humorous comic-style illustrations of more than 35 Missourians who made a contribution to the state or nation yet are largely forgotten by subsequent generations. 168 pages. Compiled by Jim Borwick and Brett Dufur. $14.95. ISBN: 0-9646625-8-2

GUIDE TO CYCLING KANSAS CITY

Seasoned cyclist's advice, maps & route information for more than 85 routes throughout Kansas City. Road routes, trails and more. 168 pages. By Steve Katz. $12.95. ISBN: 0-9632730-3-5

GUIDE TO CYCLING ST. LOUIS: SECOND EDITION

All new for 1998. The definitive cycling guide to St. Louis for road and mountain bikers. 176 pages. By Steve Katz. $15.95. ISBN: 1-891708-01-5

MISSOURI GHOSTS—SPIRITS, HAUNTS AND RELATED LORE

A lifetime collection of spirits, haunts and folklore. Highlights more than a century of Missouri's most spine-chilling and unexplainable phenomena. Fully illustrated. 230 pages. By Joan Gilbert. $14.95. ISBN: 0-9646625-7-4

RIVER VALLEY COMPANION—A NATURE GUIDE

A nice balance between nature, science and fun. This easy-to-use, richly illustrated four-season guide identifies commonly seen trees, flowers, birds, animals, insects, rocks, fossils, clouds, reptiles, footprints and more. Features the Missouri River valley's most outstanding sites and nature daytrips. 256 pages. Compiled by Brian Beatte and Brett Dufur. $14.95. ISBN: 0-9646625-1-5

SHOW ME MOUNTAIN BIKING

Comprehensive, all-new guide to 80 of the best, most scenic single-track adventures in the state. Great maps, photos and just the information we've all been waiting for. For beginners to advanced riders. 220 pages. By Brett Dufur. $16.95. ISBN: 1-891708-02-3

WIT AND WISDOM OF MISSOURI'S COUNTRY EDITORS

More than 600 pithy sayings from pioneer Missouri papers. Many of these quotes and quips date to the 19th century yet remain timely for today's readers. Richly illustrated and fully indexed to help you find that perfect quote. 168 pages. By William Taft. $14.95. ISBN: 0-9646625-3-1

Show Me Missouri books are available at many local bookstores. They can also be ordered directly from the publisher, using this form, or ordered by phone, fax or over the Internet.

Pebble Publishing also distributes 100 other books of regional interest, Rails-to-Trails, Missouri history, heritage, nature, recreation and more.

These are available through our mail-order catalog and our site *Trailside Books,* at www.trailsidebooks.com. If you would like to receive our catalog, please mail the form on this page.

Pebble Publishing, Inc.

P.O. Box 2 ❖ Rocheport, MO 65279
(800) 576-7322 ❖ Fax: (573) 698-3108

Quantity	*Book Title*	*x Unit Price = Total*

Mo. residents add 6.975% sales tax = -----------
Shipping ($3 first book, $1 each additional title) = -----------
Total = -----------

Name:_____

Email Address:_____

Address:_____ Apt._____

City, State, Zip_____

Phone: (____) _____

Credit Card # _____

Expiration Date ____/____/____ Please send catalog ____

Visit *Trailside Books* online at www.trailsidebooks.com

THE NEXT FEW PAGES INCLUDE COUPONS AND ADVERTISEMENTS IN SUPPORT OF MISSOURI CYCLISTS AND TRAILS.

PLEASE PATRONIZE THESE BUSINESSES AND ORGANIZATIONS.

NOTES:

NOTES:

NOTES:

NOTES:

— BIKE MAINTENANCE LOG: —

Date:
Work Performed:

Install Notes:

❑　Good to go!

❑　Maintenance Still Needed Before Next Ride:

Bike To Do List Within Next Month:

Sometime this Season:

By Next Season:

Buy List:

— BIKE MAINTENANCE LOG: —

Date:

Work Performed:

Install Notes:

❑ Good to go!

❑ Maintenance Still Needed Before Next Ride:

Bike To Do List Within Next Month:

Sometime this Season:

By Next Season:

Buy List:

— BIKE MAINTENANCE LOG: —

Date:
Work Performed:

Install Notes:

❑   Good to go!

❑   Maintenance Still Needed Before Next Ride:

Bike To Do List Within Next Month:

Sometime this Season:

By Next Season:

Buy List:

— BIKE MAINTENANCE LOG: —

Date:

Work Performed:

Install Notes:

❑   Good to go!

❑   Maintenance Still Needed Before Next Ride:

Bike To Do List Within Next Month:

Sometime this Season:

By Next Season:

Buy List:

RIDE LOG:

Date: Trail Name:

Weather:

List of Riders:

How Long it Takes to Get There:

Comments:

Next Time Bring:

Date: Trail Name:

Weather:

List of Riders:

How Long it Takes to Get There:

Comments:

Next Time Bring:

RIDE LOG:

Date: Trail Name:

Weather:

List of Riders:

How Long it Takes to Get There:

Comments:

Next Time Bring:

Date: Trail Name:

Weather:

List of Riders:

How Long it Takes to Get There:

Comments:

Next Time Bring:

QUICK REFERENCE
TABLE OF CONTENTS

REFER TO PAGES 6 - 9 FOR
A COMPLETE LIST OF TRAILS

THREE MORE NEW TRAILS JUST IN! SEE PAGE 223.